Praise for
PRACTICAL KABBALAH

"I think this is a superb, rich text that should be in the hands of everybody interested in furthering the understanding of the mystical aspects of their soul."

—CAROLINE MYSS,
author of *Anatomy of the Spirit* and
Why People Don't Heal

"Rabbi Laibl Wolf is a remarkable teacher who brings a wealth of contemporary understanding of psychology and humanity to his teaching of an ancient wisdom. That's what makes his Kabbalah 'practical,' and usable in our everyday lives. This wonderful book could open the door to Kabbalah to anyone with an open heart or an open mind."

—ROGER KAMENETZ,
author of *The Jew in the Lotus* and *Stalking Elijah*

"Rabbi Laibl Wolf's book is the work of an extraordinary teacher. He presents complex concepts of the Kabbalah in a way that they are easily understood even by a novice in Jewish Mysticism. More important, his vivid wording and imagery succeed in making the ideas come alive: they become acutely relevant to the readers, illuminating them with insight and meaningfulness, opening doors to untapped self-discovery and authentic spirituality."

—RABBI J. IMMANUEL SCHOCHET, PH.D.,
professor of philosophy, Toronto, Ontario;
author of *The Mystical Dimension*

PRACTICAL KABBALAH

A Guide to Jewish Wisdom for Everyday Life

RABBI LAIBL WOLF

THREE RIVERS PRESS
NEW YORK

Published by Three Rivers Press, 201 East 50th Street, New York, New York 10022. Member of the Crown Publishing Group.

Random House, Inc. New York, Toronto, London, Sydney, Auckland

www.randomhouse.com

THREE RIVERS PRESS is a registered trademark of Random House, Inc.

Printed in the United States of America

Designed by Meryl Sussman Levavi/digitext, inc.

Library of Congress Cataloging-in-Publication Data
Wolf, Laibl.
    Practical Kabbalah : a guide to Jewish wisdom for everyday life / by Laibl Wolf.
        p.   cm.
        1. Jewish way of life. 2. Kabbalah. 3. Sefirot (Kabbalah)
I. Title.
BM723.W6   1999
296.7'12—dc21   99-13940
                                                                    CIP

ISBN 0-609-80378-6

10 9 8 7 6 5 4 3 2 1

First Editon

To my wife, Leah

Contents

Contents

List of Illustrations

Acknowledgments

THERE ARE COUNTLESS individuals who have contributed to this book, and I am indebted to them all. However, in particular it would be remiss of me not to publicly acknowledge the following individuals whose support and encouragement have been a source of real inspiration. To those who have been instrumental in constructing the building blocks of my faith: my master and teacher, the Lubavitcher Rebbe, Rabbi Menachem M. Schneerson, of blessed memory; my spiritual mentor, Rabbi Shneur Zalmen Serebryanski, of blessed memory; my parents—Reb Pinchos and Regina Wolf—may they continue to live many and healthy years; my brother Don, whose acumen has always been of assistance to me. My sincere thanks to Emanuel Althaus, Morry Fraid, Efrem Harkham, Uri Harkham, Lynette and Menachem Joel, Eric Kornhauser, Moni Liberman, Garth Symond, Jeffrey Weiss, who have made the work of writing this book possible through their kindness and generosity. Adrienne Weiss of Adrienne Weiss Corporation has always extended herself and given me both practical advice and friendship, and Julie Frank of Fifty Plus Expo was the one who moved this undertaking from square one and has been invaluable, as has the energy and exuberance of Roselyn Cosentino. Thanks to my literary agent, Frank Waiman of The Literary Group, without whom this book would not have seen the light of day. My sincere thanks to the special team at Random House: Laura Wood, who was so patient with a first-time author; and Doug Pepper, with whom an immediate chemistry imbued me with confidence in a great publishing company; Jessica Schulte, who steered the book to completion; Brian Belfiglio and Ari Gersen, whose gifts of making the unknown better known have served this book so well; and Jim Walsh, for his painstaking and loving care of aesthetics and style. Thanks as well to Judith Estrine, whose talent for formulating my often convoluted sentences and obtuse grammar into something that the reader can read with lucidity and ease is appreciated. I must acknowledge some special friends—friends being as precious as pearls—Nachman and Ilana Guriel, who have kept me physically functional, and a special person whose friendship I treasure since the first grade in junior school when we first met—Arnold Rosenbaum. The Human Development Institute that I founded has been in the administrative hands of a talented and astute expatriate Australian, Rabbi Moshe Raitman, who has been solely responsible for the success of my various lecture tours, ably assisted by a special Mordechai Smith. At a time when information has become increasingly democratized and accessible, Web page managers are central to "spreading the word." Thank you, Moshe Merwitz and Yisroel Meyer, for your generosity of time and expertise.

Acharon acharon chaviv—the very last is the dearest of all. To my dear wife, Leah, and my children, Olamit and my son-in-law Eli, Yaakov and my daughter-in-law Daniella, Devorah and my son-in-law Abba, Moshe, Menachem, Chaya, and Yisroel. You have sometimes had an absent husband and father, and therefore your individual greatness is a tribute to your own gifts. Thank you for putting up with me and being so loving.

To the Creator, for providing for me with a life of fulfillment and so many wonderful opportunities to grow, discover, and share with others.

PRACTICAL KABBALAH

Introduction

Kabbalah is an ancient Jewish wisdom that explains the eternal laws of how spiritual energy moves through the Cosmos. For many centuries holy men have spent their lives immersed in the study of its mystical teachings. Library shelves are filled with thick volumes of arcane Kabbalistic commentary that illuminate tiny elements of its myriad levels of profound truth.

To truly understand the Kabbalah one must spend a lifetime committed to study and prayer. Yet even without delving deeply into its esoteric depths, the wisdom it embodies can enrich our lives in innumerable ways. In *Practical Kabbalah* we will embark on a spiritual adventure with a down-to-earth destination.

We all seek to imbue our lives with meaning and purpose. We aspire to clarity of vision and strength of conviction. Unfortunately, very few of us are born possessing the ability to act instinctively on our innate purpose.

I wrote this book to make the basic teachings of the Kabbalah relevant to daily life while at the same time providing the modern reader with a taste of the original intent. Self-understanding and personal mastery are the goals. Toward this end we will examine what the Kabbalah says regarding the nature of Mind and Heart. We will engage in simple imaging exercises and use as our guide the principles of Hassidic psychology as expressed through the school of Chabad Lubavitch Hassidism.

Practical Kabbalah is divided into two sections. The first provides a general introduction to the tradition of Kabbalah. We will look at some personalities and concepts and explore the fascinating parallels between Kabbalah and other spiritual traditions. In the second section we will study the ten spiritual flows known as the *Sefirot* that form the basic foundation of Kabbalah. Using a variety of meditation exercises and creative visualizations, we will learn how to tailor the deep knowledge of this ancient wisdom to satisfy our modern longings. We will discover how the *Sefirotic* wellsprings can guide us on our journey to spiritual growth.

Many spiritual travelers have followed the path of Kabbalah. It sustained the Jewish nation through a geographical exile of two thousand years. Even the Dalai Lama has consulted its teachers in search of the clue to the survival of his own newly exiled nation.

Until very recently, Kabbalah's profound and complex teachings were inaccessible to Western society. It was written in the ancient languages of Hebrew and Aramaic and encoded to seal its insights from untutored eyes. Nevertheless some information filtered down and found its way into other cultures and religious traditions, both East and West. As you read this book, you may recognize aspects of Kabbalah that became transposed into other traditions of belief.

Today we return to these ancient precepts. In a world that lacks self-confidence and spiritual purpose, we yearn for a system that can lead us to fulfillment. If we are to survive as sensitive, caring, and evolved human beings, we must undergo a revolution in our perception of life's meaning. We must study the success stories of those who have survived intense personal challenges and societal upheavals.

Four Keys to Growth

A case study appears within the Kabbalah's ancient pages—the survival of the Jewish people in exile. Historically no other people have suffered such prolonged adversity and yet enjoyed such disproportionate personal success in host societies. What is the key to this extraordinary history?

Scholars who study the mystical writings of this ancient people have distilled four guiding principles that enabled the Jews as a people to survive and flourish. From them we can extrapolate our own keys with which to nurture the seeds of change and personal growth.

THE FOUR KEYS TO CHANGE

Emunah: You must <u>believe</u> that you can change.

Ratzon: You must draw upon strength of <u>personal will.</u>

Avodah: You must <u>practice</u> a program of insight.

Oneg: You must <u>experience the joy</u> of success.

Kabbalah explores the mysterious labyrinths of altered states and higher spiritual realms. Within its teachings lie the tools to tame the ego mind and harness haphazard emotions. In *Practical Kabbalah* we will interpret esoteric principles and apply them to our everyday lives.

We will learn that the key to happiness lies in our ability to draw from our positive side at the moment of choice. Even seeming adversities have a positive flipside, the proverbial blessing in disguise. But it is only through the exercise of wise choice that the blessing will reveal itself.

All events possess redeeming virtues—if we choose wisely. Everything that happens in our lives is a lesson to be learned. We can choose to interpret "reality" empathically or from a self-centered, narrow point of view.

The process of self-observation and self-scrutiny (*avoido*) is described in Hassidic psychology as *cheshbon nefesh,* which literally means becoming a "soul accountant." The arena for *cheshbon nefesh* is the ordinary: the mundane, earthly realm of human endeavor. As a well-known mystical instruction in the Talmud states, life's teaching "is no longer in heaven," but in the moment, here on earth.

We discover in the Kabbalah that the world doesn't change of its own volition. Our personal transformation alters the shape of the Cosmos, not the other way around. We are responsible for effecting change in the Cosmos, and it is profoundly enabling when one comes to truly understand that the Cosmos seeks our well-being.

It is written that before we came into the world we were all-knowing. At birth an angel came and "filed" our insights into our subconscious mind. Now the aim of life's journey is to draw upon these intuitive insights and enrich the world with their expression. The Cosmos elicits these inner truths from us by offering up challenges upon which we can grow in wisdom. The mystics of Kabbalah teach that just as the grape produces wine when pressed, and the olive produces oil when pounded, so should we, when challenged, come forth with wisdom. But wisdom requires that we approach life with faith, discipline, and an open mind.

Sometimes life appears to be like a journey through a desert of greed, insecurity, and fear. But we can choose what we see: in the seemingly inert desert, life teems beneath the dry sands. Wait for night to fall and you will discover the nocturnal fauna. Look in the right places and you will find determined flora. And beneath the surface flow subterranean streams of living waters. Similarly, the same people who grasp, withhold, and threaten also possess an inner core of goodness that seeks the light of day. Each of us has the potential to share our insight and guidance and to elicit it from others. But first we must find the wisdom within ourselves.

The Cave

Rabbi Shimon bar Yochai, the scholar who compiled the Zohar, (the "Book of Splendor—the repository of the major Kabbalistic teachings), was forced to hide from powerful Roman inquisitors, who were so afraid of his Kabbalistic teachings that they saw in him a threat to the entire Roman Empire. Bar Yochai eventually emerged from the cave where he had lived for many years, and he beamed the light of Zoharic teachings on the generations that followed.

Each of us must discover how to emerge from our personal cave of constricting darkness and allow our uniqueness to illuminate the lives of those fated to share our journey. Only ego stands in the way of sharing our gifts, expressing compassion, and discovering the positive side of adversity.

The Kabbalah tells us that the more giving we are, the more our inner storehouses become replenished—with warmth, happiness, and inner peace. They appear on their own so that we don't need to lunge for the sweet things in life. When we give to others we create the space within for a beneficent Cosmos to replenish us.

In *Practical Kabbalah* I have tried to provide you with the tools with which to reinterpret reality. We will discover how to reshape our world by creating a revolution in our relationships. Our objective is to achieve the universal goals of

FULFILLMENT: The balance of mind and emotion.

SECURITY AND INNER PEACE: The faith with which to vanquish fear. The capacity to embrace inner strength, wholeness, and serenity.

LOVE AND COMPASSION: The emotional connections that bond people in warm, empathic, and committed relationships.

HONEST AND CONFIDENT EXPRESSION: The mastery of words, behavior, and thought, so that they become an expression of our inner truth and uniqueness.

If these goals are universal, why do so many of us fail to achieve them in our personal and professional lives?

The answer lies in our understanding of the true nature of the Mind and Emotion.

According to the Kabbalah, Mind consists of a series of three spiritual energies that the physical brain mediates. These energies create enlightenment and understanding. Emotion consists of seven energies that manifest through the heart. Together they are the ten *Sefirot*, the spiritual energies that flow through the body.

On a Personal Note

Whenever I read a book, especially one that is trying to teach spiritual insights, I am always curious about the author. What is the author's life experience? Where did the author study, and with whom? What is the author's reason for publishing? Therefore allow me to share a little of my life's story with you.

I am the son and son-in-law of Holocaust survivors. Like all children of survivors, I am self-conscious about being alive. I am deeply aware that I might never have been born—at least not to the parents who brought me into the world. As a child, I found a book that graphically depicted the unspeakable horrors of concentration camp life. Late at night I would lie in bed and re-create in my mind scenes from the text. Even more traumatic were my parents' anguished nightmare screams as they relived the Holocaust in their dreams.

What haunted me as a child continues to haunt me today. Would I have had the will to survive? Or would cowardice have afforded me a simple way out—to give up and die?

Fate played a cruel trick on my parents. They survived, but their parents, grandparents, brothers, and sisters were murdered in the gas chambers. Yet these survivors somehow drew strength and conviction from a hidden resource—an inner fountain of life. They did not rage against a G-d who silently witnessed the absolute degradation of humanity; or against a Cosmos that bred cultured monsters, Ph.D.s with a taste for good music and torture, kindness to animals and bestial brutality toward humans.

Instead my parents and in-laws married, bore children, and brazenly stared down Western society. They even went on to achieve economic and social success. Unbelievably, they remained true to the G-d who suffered with them in Auschwitz, Bergen-Belsen, and Treblinka. How did they patch-quilt their broken bodies, broken minds, and broken hearts? From where did they summon the will to live and even the audacity to bring new lives into an uncertain world?

Pause a moment. Recall an instant in time when you were genuinely terrified. It may have occurred in real life or in a dream. Relive that moment. Stand outside yourself and observe your mind. Where are your thoughts— those "monkey thoughts" that jump around at the beck and call of your emotions? Where are your feelings? You might admit to yourself that in the terror of the moment you lost control. Your inner balance dissolved. An unnamable force seemed to hold you in its grip. Close your eyes and relive the experience.

Now think about the hundreds of thousands of survivors of senseless violence and terror throughout the world, who live nightly with the memory of horrendous demons overpowering them yet somehow, impossibly, go on to lead conventional lives of relative balance, discipline, and even faith.

Herein lies the secret I want to share and explore with you: the will to survive and the quest for meaning—the greatest of life's mysteries. Through my study of the Kabbalah I have gained profound insights into the nature of human motivation, and I now understand how my parents managed to continue to live in the wake of unprecedented calamity.

Twenty-eight years ago I was taken under the wing of a wise man. His name was Reb Zalmen Serebryanski, of blessed memory. He too was a Holocaust survivor and a new immigrant to Australia. He was a cultured and well-known scholar and an extraordinary teacher. He was also a Hassid, and as I learned, Hassidism holds the key to understanding the Kabbalah. He taught me many things, but the source that directed me on my life's journey was his teaching of Hassidic psychology. His insight and wisdom sowed the seeds of my own growth and development. It was he who introduced me to the teacher who was to become my master, the Lubavitcher Rebbe.

I spent years engaged in intense study and strict discipline, struggling to experience the joy of enlightenment. During those same years I studied law and graduate work in educational psychology. I taught in high school and university and became a counselor and chaplain to university students in the United States and Australia. I became a lecturer and seminar leader and traveled more than a million miles around the world. Somewhere in between I helped to rear seven children— an endeavor that succeeded only because of the gifts and forbearance of a very special woman, Leah, my wife of twenty-nine years.

In the course of my travels I developed close ties with people from all cultures, religions, and walks of life. I have been honored to meet with spiritual teachers, spiritual seekers from both the East and the West, hard-nosed business executives, psychiatrists and psychologists, child care professionals, and many others, all striving to put together the puzzle of life.

It is they who first gave me the idea of writing a book. At first I was hesitant, but I received encouragement from my master, the late Lubavitcher Rebbe, Menachem M. Schneerson, of blessed memory. He urged me to seize the opportunity to lend direction to humanity's spiritual quest as we approach a new millennium.

You are standing at the threshold of a new path. Be courageous. Summon up the commitment you need to see it through. You are about to embark on a journey along an ancient road. It was the road taken by the People of the Book through countless generations. It has also provided the spiritual impetus for the major world religions. Yet the Kabbalah still remains enshrouded in mystery, and its contributions are not readily apparent.

You will discover how to integrate the insight and wisdom contained in the Kabbalah into your life. The result will be balanced and deeply bonded relationships. You will have an effective life, one of joy and serenity.

May my humble contribution help pave the way for all of us to sing a new song of personal and world redemption.

A Word About Chabad Hassidism

Chabad Hassidism, the theology and transpersonal psychology that explains and decodes the ancient Kabbalah, seeks our physical, emotional, and mental well-being. It demonstrates that person and Cosmos are complementary and synergistic aspects of one greater Whole. It teaches that what we think, say, or do leaves a mark on the universe. And the changed universe "communicates" with us in the new "language" that includes our contribution.

Kabbalah is deeply mystical, but its Hassidic explanations provide surprisingly practical approaches to the challenges of daily life. At a time when modern society is searching for ways to free itself from dissension and personal estrangement, this ancient tradition provides contemporary answers.

PART ONE

SPIRIT MOVE

1

Abraham—
The Rebel Mystic

You may have read somewhere that Kabbalah is a mystical phenomenon that emerged from the medieval period of history, a thirteenth-century creation. This is only part of the story. The academic texts tell us that Moses de Lyon published the major text of Kabbalah, known as the Zohar (the Inner Light), in the medieval period. However, Rabbi Shimon bar Yochai had already handwritten this work a thousand years earlier in ancient Israel. And he had written it on the basis of an oral tradition that went back another seventeen hundred years.

The Kabbalah of the Torah (the body of law and instruction that provides structure to Jewish society and personal spiritual disciplines for its members) is incredibly old and can be traced back to Abraham, who is credited with having composed Kabbalistic works. But even predating this, we know that Noah and Adam were fully conversant with its teachings.

The Kabbalah is enshrouded in mystery. Today academics still debate how it may have evolved and how its spirit moved through the centuries. I have not set out to write a history book or analysis of theological writings. At the same time, it is necessary to provide a brief background so the reader understands the roots of Kabbalah. The interpretation that follows is gleaned from mystical writings. Some learned academics may differ with this view, but my teachers assure me that what follows resonates with the Cosmic truths contained in the holy texts.

Abraham was tall and gaunt. The desert sands had sharpened his facial features into fractured contours. An imposing and stoic figure, he impressed those around him with his regal bearing and the clarity of his vision. He was the most celebrated leader in the Middle East.

Despite the trappings of obvious wealth and comfort, Abraham lived a spartan life. He took meticulous care of his flocks of sheep and even more so of his shepherds. After all, he too was a shepherd. Nicknamed the *Ivri* (the Hebrew), Abraham was a living legend throughout the land. He was a shepherd-king and a warrior of renown. But most of all he was known as the wise mystic who had an altogether strange notion of a single Deity. He could summon powers from Above to decimate an army or heal a sick child, and he saw things that others could not see. Angelic forces whispered in his ear. It was known that he received instructions from the mysterious G-d.

Let us imagine Abraham standing on the sand hill, the desert Tel, thinking of days gone by. He recalls the rebelliousness of his youth; how he challenged the idolatrous ways of Mesopotamian polytheism; how he was thrown into the fiery furnace by the Mesopotamian king and defied all the laws of nature by surviving the intense heat without a blemish. Then came the transforming instructions from Above, when G-d ordered Abraham to leave the country of his birth and travel to a strange land.

We see him now, standing in that new land, holy energy vibrating through his body. This land will one day be named after his grandson Israel. Until the end of days it will remain the crossroads for warring armies that seek dominion of their faith.

When Abraham heeded G-d's order he was already fully proficient in what was to become known as Kabbalah. He had even authored a major Kabbalistic text—

Sefer HaYetzira (the Book of Creative Formation). He was an acclaimed astrologer and conversant in the magic and witchcraft of the East. In his youth Abraham had turned his back on the negative forces of *tum'ah* (spiritual blemish) and adopted the pathway of spiritual monotheism. This rebellious stance earned him his calling card—the *Ivri,* meaning the "other-sider," or the "outsider." The word *Ivri* became anglicized as "Hebrew."

Academics argue about the origins of the word *Ivri.* It could have been adopted from his famous forebear of similar name, Eiver, the great-grandson of Noah. Or it might simply note that his origins were from across the Euphrates River, the other side of the proverbial tracks, hence "the other-sider." Perhaps it was simply a nasty epithet thrown at him by the ruling classes to convey their displeasure at the fast-growing popularity of this upstart. Whatever its origins, his name has been recorded for posterity.

Abraham's dreams for the success of the generations to come were pinned on his son Isaac, born of his wife, Sarah. The future of the dynasty was dependent on this loyal and unassuming son. In Isaac he detected the qualities that would steer the newly emerging Hebrews through the spiritual minefields of the East. It was to safeguard Isaac that Abraham had cast out his other sons—the sons born to him by his second wife, Hagar.

These youths had been a poor influence on Isaac, entangled as they were in the beliefs of the prevailing cults of polytheism and witchcraft.

We can imagine Abraham's sadness as he recalls their bitter parting, and his prayers as he remembers the gifts he bestowed upon them—insights and spiritual powers with which they might navigate the higher realms. If his sons were to play with the fire of idolatry, at least they would have a moral compass to guide them in a positive direction. Abraham's gifts would allow them to see the nature of evil—*shem hatum'ah,* the dark side of higher reality. Would they use their knowledge wisely? He didn't know. He only hoped that these teachings would hold them in good stead as they departed for the land of the East—the biblical code name for Hodu—India.

And here we find the beginnings of the great encounter between the East and the future West. It makes understandable the remarkable parallels between mystical Judaism and the Eastern pathways of Buddhism and Hinduism.

East Meets Early West

We conjecture that upon arrival in ancient India—Hodu—Abraham's sons began to share their insights with the indigenous peoples who even named the great river, the Indus River, after the father who sent them here. In Brahmin *Indus* means "the other-sider"—the *Ivri!* Furthermore, their Deity—*B R A H M A N,* is simply a rearrangement of the basic letters of the father's name—*A B R A H A M.* Abraham's great-grandson Ashurim was said to have created the spiritual commune known as the *ashram.* Interestingly, the Aramaic translation of the Bible, *Targum Onkelos,* translates *ashurim* as "camps" or "communes." Other Hebrew concepts began to creep into the Eastern people's belief systems. *Ram,* elevated deity in the East, in Hebrew means "elevated." *Veydah* is etymologically related to the Hebrew word for "knowledge" and "insight," *deyah. Tamas,* Indian for "impurity," is obviously the Hebrew word *tameh,* with the same meaning.

Apart from terminological similarities, we can also discern conceptual parallels. For example, a concept like reincarnation, *tulku* in the East, is the Hebrew teaching of *Gilgul HaNefesh,* the cyclical reincarnation of the wandering of the soul. *Karma,* the "baggage" carried from the previous lifetime, reminds one of the Hebrew *hashgacha pratit,* the specific cause-and-effect relationship molded by past lives. The tests and openings that constitute moments of opportunity to change one's reincarnative destiny are called *bardos* in the East and *nissyonot* in Hebrew.

Parallel Terminology and Concept

HEBREW	EAST	MEANING
Ivri	*Indus*	Other-sider
Avraham	*Brahman*	Father of nation
Deyah	*Veydah*	Knowledge
Ashurim	*Ashram*	Spiritual wealth
Ram	*Ram*	Elevated
Tamei	*Tames*	Spiritual Impurity
Gilgul	*Tulku*	Reincarnation
Hashgacha	*Karma*	Next life "baggage"
Nissayon	*Bardo*	Test, opportunity

The Nature of Breath

An interesting and significant approach to meditation in the East focuses on the science of breathing. Congruent with this is the anthropomorphic association of breath with creation as outlined in the Hebrew Bible: "And He breathed the living soul into his [Adam's] nose." The Hebrew word for "breath" is *neshima*, while the word for "soul" is *neshama*. The connection is obvious. Focusing on breath is focusing on the life force itself. The *Hassidic* masters of Kabbalah offered the meditational imagery of G-d's investiture in the world as the process of *memalleh*—the *filling* of the world with G-dly presence, just like breath filling the lungs.

Emptying the mind, which is another Eastern meditational teaching, is akin to the Kabbalistic teaching that the world derives from a void, an emptiness known as *halal*. (Is this the progenitor of the Greek *hyle*, which means "the basic material from which the Cosmos was sculpted"?) Emptying the mind creates the basis for the contemplative filling process, *memalleh*, known in Hassidic meditation as *hitbonenut*.

The Kabbalah does not teach that the "science of breath" is an end in itself, nor the emptying of the mind a virtue in its own right. Rather, they are disciplines that lead to greater insight and are instructed by defined devotional practices.

The Early Kabbalists

Abraham was proficient in what was to become known much later as Kabbalah. He often called upon its mystical powers as well as its practical wisdom. The shepherd-king had studied in the great spiritual teaching center known as the Academy of Shem and Eiver, established by Noah's son Shem (the father of the *Shemites*, or Semitic peoples) and Shem's own grandson Eiver, who was Abraham's forebear.

The Academy of Shem and Eiver was not a public center of learning. Its portals were restricted to the early initiates—those destined to carry the spiritual teachings of a future Torah in its early path through the desert. The Hebrew patriarchs, Abraham, Isaac, and Jacob, were tutored in this academy. Jacob reputedly studied these esoteric spiritual disciplines for fourteen years. The architects of the Jewish nation thus acquired a spiritual discipline that was to become the hallmark of the future People of the Book. Jacob's son Judah reopened the academy in the very heart of ancient Egypt, and it continued to function secretly throughout the four hundred years of exile and slavery in Egypt, even in the presence of Ramses II himself.

Yet Abraham was not the first Kabbalist. The knowledge of the spiritual forces that constitute the Cosmos and maintain its physical and spiritual integrity were already known to the first Person—Adam. And herein lie some fascinating teachings.

So let us leave Abraham, the first Hebrew, and visit the dawning of the very first millennium in the person of Adam, also known as *Harishon* ("the First One").

The Letters of Creation

Who was this two-legged humanoid who stared down all other creatures? Was he/she/it human? Kabbalah informs us that Adam, primordial Person, was initially a man-woman composite—an androgynous being. Only later was Adam split into two, the predominant masculine component located in Adam and the feminine in Eve. Even today man possesses latent femininity, and woman, latent masculinity. The masculine-feminine duality encompasses all of creation. Even the Hebrew letters upon which we will be meditating contribute to essentially masculine and feminine components of language. Ultimately these letters relate to masculine and feminine spiritual forces.

In the mystical tradition of Kabbalah, an individual's feminine component is more prophetic, prescient, and gifted in spiritual skills. Hence the patriarchs' wives, Sarah, Rebecca, Rachel, and Leah, were spiritually gifted. Even the G-dly presence that envelopes the prophet is called the feminine *Shechina* (indwelling).

Yet the concepts of masculinity and femininity are not absolute. Man and woman can exhibit both masculine and feminine expressions. This duality operates throughout nature. Earth is feminine and accepts the masculine activity of people—both men and women—of seeding the soil and nourishing the seed, giving rise to progeny—the harvest.

The spiritual energies that define Mind and Emotion possess masculine and feminine properties, and throughout the Kabbalah we find gender imagery. This will be discussed in detail in part 2.

In truth, Adam was not really human like you and me. His connection to the nature of creation was literally "out of this world." He intuited the twenty-two creative forces that shape the universe and understood the separate paths they took in entering the realm of the "here and now." With this understanding he transposed the mystical pathways he saw into twenty-two distinct shapes. Each became a letter in the Hebrew alphabet.

Adam also understood the energies associated with each of these letters. He replicated their individual energies through the breath as it rose from his lungs, impinging on the larynx—and then becoming shaped as sounds through the five aspects of his mouth: the lips, tongue, teeth, palate, and throat. This resulted in twenty-two sounds—the various sounds of the Hebrew alphabet. Adam used the articulation of sound to express the depth and beauty of life.

Each letter of the Hebrew language is a window into a higher reality. The letters constitute a language known as *Lashon HaKodesh*—"the Holy Tongue"—Hebrew. That is why the Kabbalah places great emphasis on the analysis of words and letters, their numerical equivalence, interchangeability, shapes, and the end-of-word final letters. Each nuance opens up a panorama of spiritual depth, far more complex than any grammatical construct might suggest.

Consider a simple exercise. The word for "wanting"

or "desiring" (*ratzah*) is made up of the three Hebrew consonants that make the sounds R-TZ-H. These three consonants also form the basis of the word meaning "the adversary" (*hatzar*)—H-TZ-R. Further still, another word made up of these three consonants—TZ-H-R—means "clarity" or "enlightenment" (*Tzohar*—also Anglicized as *Zohar*). A fourth combination of these three consonants is TZ-R-H, meaning "trouble" or "constraints" *(tzarah).* In English these words seem unrelated. But in Kabbalah the fact that these words possess the same root letters means that they are inherently connected.

So we learn that directing our *will* and *desire* incorrectly creates an internal *adversary*—that is, trouble—within and without. Directing it correctly brings *enlightenment* and *clarity* of spirit.

If the letters of the Hebrew alphabet are symbols depicting the basic spiritual components of creation, then their combination as the *Torah* provides a total blueprint of that creation. Let us explore this blueprint and learn more about the spiritual aspects of creation.

2

The Blueprint of the Cosmos

The Torah tells us that millions of people resided at the foothills of the Sinai mountain—the population of a modern metropolis. Each person there witnessed something that transformed the world. It marked the beginning of the Judaic tradition, offshoots of which became Christianity and Islam. It also gave birth to the tradition of Kabbalah.

On that humble-size mountain, Moshe Rabbeinu (Moses) addressed the citizens of a new nation—the nation of Israel. He taught them the Torah. The Torah was a national constitution and personal manual. But its deeper import was that it contained the blueprint of creation and provided the cord that tied G-d to the People of the Book.

Like any constitution or code, it had to be interpreted. Moses educated his people at four levels—each level decrypting another layer. Each person there learned the basic meaning of the rules that govern personal behavior, social consciousness, code of ethics, and lifestyle and relationship with their Creator. This level of instruction became known as *Peshat,* meaning "Plain, Unadorned, Stripped of Complication."

The second round of "lectures" was limited to those whose capacities enabled them to fathom the underlying implications of the *Peshat* level. This level investigated the deeper allusions that were only hinted at in the text. Known as the *Remez* level, it alludes to a deeper layer of intent within the basic information.

The third session was highly restricted, and the prerequisites for participation were demanding. This select group was taught the deeper *Derush* ("Inferred") level of the same Torah. For example, sometimes you may find yourself trying to convey a concept, but its complexity and depth make its literal expression impossible. You might resort to an appropriate analogy, or metaphor, or perhaps an allegory. Although imperfect, a clever analogy encompasses the essence that needs to be conveyed.

At the same time that it illuminates, an analogy obscures, because it is couched in an example that is usually quite unlike the intended information. Yet, ironically, by *hiding* the information in an analogy, you actually *reveal* its essence. This is what *Derush* does. It makes the essence of Torah known via metaphors and tales. To the sages they become the keys to hidden meanings. A whole body of Torah literature known as Midrash is devoted to the *Derush* form of teaching.

And we haven't even reached the Kabbalah level. This took place when Moshe then chose a handful of future *nistarim*—(literally "hidden ones") and taught them the *Sod* ("Secret") level of the Torah. At this level tangible reality is reduced to symbolism, numerology, and spiritual forces—the ethereal energy that underlies creation. This hidden teaching was "received" (*kibel*) from generation to generation—hence the name *Kabbalah* (the process of receiving).

PARDES—THE ORCHARD OF KABBALAH MYSTICISM

P	*Peshat*	Plain Meaning
R	*Remez*	Hint, Allusion
D	*Derush*	Derivation via Analogy, Metaphor
S	*Sod*	Secret, the Kabbalah

The Spiritual Genetic Code

The traditional approach to the study of history assumes that historical process is the product of events impinging upon an era, or of charismatic leaders leaving their mark on society. My spiritual mentor, the Lubavitcher Rebbe, offered a deeper spiritual insight. He noted that it is also affected by the vertical dimension—that of spirituality. In other words, spiritual dynamics affect history.

Consider a dramatic example. The Industrial Revolution, the beginnings of scientific method, the rise of nascent nationalism in Europe, the growth of Puritanism in England, and the emergence of Hassidism all evolved within a remarkably short time span. This might seem a historical coincidence. Yet the social, economic, and religious developments in the respective parts of the Western world where these phenomena took place were far from identical. It would seem as if some common inner force propelled each of these geographically disparate historical developments into the world.

Furthermore the date for a historical transformation was predicted in the Zohar, the text of which was first recorded some fifteen hundred years earlier. The Zohar noted that a time would come when the "fountains of knowledge" would burst open from above and below, forever changing the landscape of the world. In other words, beyond the social and economic forces at work lay a universal spiritual dynamic that coalesced these separate factors into an integrated whole.

Just as human genes move the adult-child from gangling youth into maturity, so too historical events often arise as the inevitable consequence of a cosmic double helix. One's own progression through life is not solely the product of personal initiative and training. That initiative itself is the result of a defining spiritual aura—the soul. Just note how the 1960s and early 1970s were the result of youthful reformist zeal seeking the transformation of society and personal expression. Contrast it with the later 1970s and 1980s, which gave rise to a self-centeredness and an ethic of greed. The 1990s have yet again seen a further spiritual shift, a further turning inward. These transitions are not easy to explain. A deep spiritual dynamic appears to be at work, encoded within the Torah—the blueprint of creation.

Works recently published based on mathematical constructs have pointed to a "hidden spiritual code" within the Torah. From a Kabbalistic point of view, even these works fall far short of explaining the spiritual dynamics at play in the Cosmos.

The Cosmic Kiss

The metaphor of breath is used extensively in the Torah's account of the creation. For example, it describes how Adam was created in two stages. The Creator initially formed Adam's physical body and only then *breathed* life into him. The Kabbalah speaks of G-d' s breath being the life force that sustains all levels of existence: the inanimate, vegetable, animal, human, and unembodied angelic beings and souls. The Creator is intimate with Its creatures. It loves them and seeks their complete benefit. The "cosmic breath" is referred to as the process of *memalleh* (filling the void), thereby animating it. As the Creator meets Its creatures face-to-face, Its breath passes between them by way of a "kiss."

When your soul merges with the divine flow of history, the Kabbalah describes it as a "cosmic kiss." The Creator and Its creations share the "cosmic breath." Breathing consciously, with awareness, can become a powerful tool for reclaiming inner balance and personal equilibrium. It can also induce altered states of consciousness, which facilitate deeper self-realization and imprint behavioral transformation.

Who Am I?

Neither your body nor your mind and heart is the essence of who you are. In Kabbalah the spiritual center is called the *neshama*. The *neshama* is the spiritual and transcendental umbilical cord conducting the life force that animates you. You might call it "soul," but it is not the soul that a Christological perception has formulated. You probably think of a soul as some deep point within. This concept is quite foreign to Jewish mystical teachings.

In Kabbalah the soul transcends four parallel realms known as *Olamot*. (See the illustration on page 36.) Our consciousness is located where the *neshama* flow intersects the lowest realm—the realm of *Assiya*. *Assiya* is the realm of time, space, and consciousness. The journey of the soul through these four realms imbues it with transcendent properties. Looking at it from a psychological perspective, you might say that the flow of *neshama* through these higher realms constitutes the subconscious.

We are really a soul-body duality. When we feel well, totally alive and glowing from head to foot, our spiritual and physical dimensions are fully integrated. When we are ill, the mind is dull and our movements are sluggish. Spiritually this denotes a slight disintegration of our spiritual and physical aspects.

Who Am I?

EIN
SOF

ATZILUT

Spiritual Umbilical Cord ⟶

BERIYA

YETZIRA

ASSIYA

Time-Space
Consciousness

When we sleep, we experience a more profound dislocation and disintegration of our inner duality. We
seemingly lose consciousness, and our soul is even more
dislocated from the body. Through our dreams we become, albeit imperfectly, conscious of the higher realms
and our presence within them.

If we were to lapse into true unconsciousness, the
dislocation of soul from body would be even greater, to
the extent that the soul would have very limited expression through the body.

The most profound disintegration of the soul-body
duality occurs at death. Here the dislocation of soul from
body is so intense that only a tenuous relationship is
maintained. But Kabbalah teaches that even in death a
basic level of integration still exists, and the body retains
its physical form. The body's progressive decay is really
the loosening of this final bond.

Recordings of near death experiences have provided
us with a window into the nature of the soul-body duality. In certain ways the near death phenomenon is similar
to some meditative states and out-of-body experiences
described in Kabbalistic literature. The founder of the
Hassidic movement, Rabbi Yisrael Ba'al Shem Tov (literally "Possessor of the Good Name"), records in a letter
to his brother-in-law, Rabbi Gershon Kittiver, how on
one occasion he practiced the altered state known as
Aliyat HeNeshama—the ascension of the soul through

the higher *Olamot* realms. He describes rising amid light and splendor, passing through a series of chambers, until he finally meets the Master Being known as *Moshiach* (Messiah), who instructs him to spread the Hassidic teachings of Kabbalah as the way to bring final realization to creation. Upon his return into the here and now, he is infused with fervor and launches the spread of Kabbalistic insights through the emergence of the Hassidic movement. During the experience his body lay prone, unmoving, and seemingly devoid of life.

The near death phenomenon raises the question of who is doing the seeing and hearing. It can't be the body lying on the operating table, its clinical death registered by the flat line on a monitor. Nor was it the Ba'al Shem Tov's body that saw and spoke with *Moshiach*. Kabbalah teaches that the "I," the essence of personality and awareness, is the "seeing and hearing" *neshama*. It remains spiritually conscious and aware.

Herein lies a major difference between many of the beliefs of the East and the Jewish mystical tradition. While *Kabbalah* acknowledges that there is much to gain from higher insights induced by altered states, our real purpose is to master the processes of conscious and deliberate thinking, speaking, and acting, right here on the earthly plane of *Assiya*. Kabbalah teaches us to integrate body and soul, by living fully in the "real" world and infusing ourselves with a deep awareness of our role as co-creators of an unfinished Cosmos. Only through this endeavor can we encounter the true "I."

Consider the great personalities of our time: Gandhi, Schweitzer, Mother Teresa, Einstein. Their greatness was manifest not in glorious spiritual reveries, but in the fusion of their higher selves with the work of their hands.

The greatness of the Lubavitcher Rebbe does not lie solely in his many miracles. His legacy includes the innumerable instances of concern he demonstrated for the material welfare of an impoverished and otherwise unknown individual on the other side of the globe.

This is the true message of Kabbalah. One doesn't have to be a full-time saint to achieve greatness. Greatness can be achieved through the communication of empathy or a wise word. In Hassidic teachings we learn that the purpose of the descent of any one soul may be simply to do one benevolent act for one other person. When the soul has completed this act, its reason for being on an earthly plane may be fully achieved. We may practice for a whole lifetime in order to meet the challenge of one singular test that determines our soul's journey in the next lifetime. Does this sound Eastern? It is an ancient Kabbalistic teaching.

Ordinary lives can transform creation itself.

3

❧

Who Are the Kabbalists?

Many people ask me what a Kabbalist looks like. What does a Kabbalist really do? It may surprise many to learn that the term is an invention of academic circles looking at the Jewish mystical tradition from the outside. The correct term for one who devotes his life to Kabbalah is *mekubal,* meaning "one who has been received." Today the term Kabbalist seems to be used liberally to describe anyone who claims to have studied some Kabbalah from a secondary work and purports to be a teacher.

There are few public *mekubalim* (plural of *mekubal*) in the world. The few who do receive people and provide assistance live in Israel or in New York, the primary centers of Jewish life.

A number of the Hassidic masters, called *rebbes,* are also proficient in Kabbalah and have considerable power. *Rebbes,* the Hassidic spiritual masters, should be distinguished from *rabbis.* The former are leaders of Hassidic movements and often are Kabbalists as well. The latter are generally community religious leaders and functionaries attached to a synagogue or temple community and are almost never Kabbalists.

It must be understood that Kabbalah is not a movement, but a spiritual mastery. Hassidism, on the other hand, is a movement, and it expounds the teachings of Kabbalah, often using a behavioral approach, as does *Chabad Lubavitch* Hassidism, to assist people in their daily lives.

Hassidism arose in eighteenth-century Europe amid abject poverty and rampant anti-Semitism. During those years Jewish society was divided into a scholastic elite and the vast majority of Jews who had very limited access to their literary heritage. It was a joyless period, characterized by an external religious fervor that often lacked truly spiritual underpinnings. Hassidism arose as a spiritual movement, democratizing Jewish society by allowing the untutored artisan to feel as close to G-d as the most celebrated scholar, and injecting joy into religious expression.

Hassidism's primary contribution remains in its adoption of a behavioral approach to Kabbalah. It teaches the applications of deep mystical teachings for the benefit of people in everyday life.

Kabbalah also offers spiritual advice, quite independent of any intervention by Kabbalists, for maintaining wellness and effecting recovery. This includes advice to ensure that all *mezuzot* (which contain an extract from the Torah that is handwritten on parchment in Hebrew and placed on the doorpost) or *teffilin* (phylacteries worn daily by an adult Jewish male, usually during morning prayers) are checked for scribal errors or normal or abnormal "wear and tear." Many of these spiritual maintenance measures were codified in conventional Jewish law. Most people are unaware of their source in Kabbalah.

Unfortunately, in the current spiritual "marketplace," you can find self-proclaimed Kabbalists who are not even conversant with the basic Jewish law and lore and who might not even practice the traditional religious *mitzvot* (literally "commandments"; used colloquially to denote acts of kindness and good deeds) as well as some who cannot even read Hebrew or Aramaic, the languages in which the Kabbalah was written.

Kabbalah is not just knowledge. It must be accompanied by a specific and highly disciplined lifestyle of a religious Jew, living the life of Torah. It is a life that imbues the ordinary with intense spirituality. One can't aspire to be a Kabbalist. It is the product of a lengthy spiritual apprenticeship and a process that invokes in the student both trepidation and a sense of awe and spiritual responsibility. Even at the end of the arduous process, a gift must be bestowed from Above to imbue the individual with supernatural powers. The tools are forged in spiritual fire. Therefore, approaching a Hassidic *rebbe* or Kabbalist can be an awesome experience. The *rebbe* can see right through to your soul. There are no secrets.

People have misconceptions about Kabbalists. They believe that Kabbalists dress in black frock coats, variously called *kapotes* or *bekeshes,* grow lengthy earlocks, wear long white socks, and parade an assortment of headgear ranging from the fur *shtreimels* or *spoticks* to the wide-brimmed "raincatchers." This stereotype is not only misleading, but is often attributed exclusively to a media-inspired category called ultra-Orthodox Jews. Even this term is misleading and simplistic. The term ultra-Orthodox is in itself a product of a judgmental approach conveying a notion of excessive religious fervor, as if this can some way be established objectively. An individual's form of garb is often less a description of religious practice than an expression of specific traditional and cultural mores rooted in history. It is a matter of custom. These dress customs apply almost equally to

Hassidic and non-Hassidic practitioners, though most wear this traditional garb only on the *Shabbos* (Sabbath). Many very religious groups wear conventional clothes throughout the week. Some Middle Eastern religious Jews dress in traditional caftan and turban, though this is a small and fast-disappearing sector of Israeli society. The same holds true for Middle Eastern Kabbalists. Most *rebbe*s, however, and some of their followers wear the traditional garb throughout the week.

What do Kabbalists do for a living? Traditionally many were artisans and tradespersons, especially in eighteenth- and nineteenth-century Europe. Some Middle Eastern exponents continue in the tradition to this day.

Today a handful of publicly accessible Kabbalists and Hassidic *rebbes* will receive people who seek their advice and assistance around the clock. They are supported by their followers and also through generous contributions or acknowledgments for the sessions. The lifestyle is rigorous—many sleep only a couple of hours a night, using the night hours for intense study of Torah at all of its levels, especially the esoteric level. They are revered, and in the case of the Hassidic *rebbes,* their word is law and instruction.

Many people turn to these "miracle workers" for healing, and each Kabbalist has his individual modality. Often the ordinary and commonplace advice he gives obscures the true source of the healing. For example, some Kabbalists advise eating a particular fruit or lighting a candle. What is not evident to the recipient of this advice is that the Kabbalist is actually focusing G-dly spiritual energy. The fruit or candle becomes the physical conduit through which spiritual energy can flow. Were the fruit to remain uneaten or the candle untouched, the Kabbalist's blessing would have no effect. This is called "building a *keili*" (a container to hold the blessing). There are Kabbalists who "read *mezuzot.*" These Kabbalists can perceive all aspects of a person's life through the *mezuzah* and offer advice based on what they find. Others recognize the soul through the person's name and that of the mother. Yet others will simply ask you to open a page of Psalms.

Many Hassidic *rebbes* hide the miraculous in the ordinary. The late Lubavitcher Rebbe, of blessed memory, often camouflaged his miraculous gifts in "ordinary" advice. He might advise a suffering individual to see a particular doctor or to undertake a specific home therapy. Somehow his advice resulted in the spontaneous remission of a serious illness. At other times the *Rebbe* simply intimated that the person would be healed—and that was enough. And at yet other times he instructed the person "to make a *l'chaim*" (to have an alcoholic drink, usually a shot of vodka, and wish the person *l'chaim*—"to life"), and it would suffice to effect a cure. Or he would take the person's Hebrew name and the name of his or her mother

SPIRITUAL LEADERS

The author with his master,
the Lubavitcher Rebbe.

The author with the
Chief Rabbi of the
British Commonwealth,
Rabbi Jonathan Sacks.

The author with the Dalai Lama.

46

to the graveside of his saintly father-in-law (his spiritual predecessor), seeking heavenly intervention.

The famous Kabbalist of the Middle East known as *Baba Sali*, of blessed memory, who died only a few decades ago, effected miraculous cures of seriously ill hospitalized patients. Under the watchful eye of doctors he instructed the patient to sip a little water. The doctors' responses of amazement and awe are on record.

Some Kabbalists, and most of the Hassidic *rebbes*, hold court, and rules of etiquette guide the relationship between them and their followers or visitors. Protocol may involve specific times for public teaching or ceremonial gatherings and dictate styles of communication, whether orally or in writing. Protocol also promotes a sense of majesty and holiness. In some instances one does not touch the *rebbe* even to shake hands upon meeting, and one always stands in his presence.

The Kabbalist is on quite another wavelength—literally out of this world—and that world is generally unknown to anyone but his followers. If you ever have an opportunity to have an audience with a Kabbalist, it could change your life.

Although this book is not a layman's manual for becoming a *mekubal*, the basic teachings of Kabbalah, as expounded through Hassidic teachings, contain insights and practical applications that can be accessed by all of us, no matter what our station in life or daily challenges. At the same time that Kabbalah explores the dizzy heights of the upper worlds, the angelic realms, and the forces that shape the Cosmos, it also provides us with the dynamics of life down here. The physical world is a finite image of the infinite realms. Hence the insights of the spiritual workings "up there" provide parallel insights into our workings "down here." The beneficent nature of creation becomes the template for positive thinking and a model for our own faith and optimism. The ultimate unity of forces in the Cosmos becomes the ideal for meaningful and loving relationships and balance right here on earth.

PART TWO

FLOWS OF MIND AND EMOTION

4

The Ten Sefirot

The Ba'al Shem Tov once told his disciples a story about a beautiful bird that flew into the king's garden and perched on the high branch of a tree. Every day the bird sang its song, and the melody so captivated the king that he vowed to capture it and bring it inside the castle to sing for him alone. The king drew his servants together and instructed them to create a human ladder via which he would reach the treetop. They did as he ordered, and all went well, until he reached out to snatch the bird. At that moment, the man at the bottom became tired and moved away. The human ladder collapsed.

What does this story tell us? On one level it is a parable that might point to the folly of trying to capture for one man's personal pleasure the bounty that was meant for us all to enjoy. But we are told that the Ba'al Shem Tov had a deeper lesson in mind. He wanted us to understand that G-d's love can descend to earth only when we support each other—the strong helping the weak and the weak aspiring to strength. When even one person gives in to weakness—to greed or cruelty—the entire structure collapses. Thus the universe is dependent upon each of our efforts.

The Kabbalah tells us that the creation is not complete. We create the environment through which the universe can be perfected. The tools we are given are the ten *Sefirot*. They are the spiritual energies of Mind and Emotion.

The Star of David

Throughout this book, we will engage in several imaging exercises that involve the image of the Star of David. The Star of David is comprised of two sets of overlapping triangles that form six points. The Kabbalah refers to them as "wings." These wings symbolize six *Sefirot* of Emotion, the flows of energy that allow us to imbue pure cerebral activity with warmth and grace. Like the wings of a bird, they propel us spiritually upward.

The overlapping triangles create twelve lines. They stand for the twelve tribes of Israel, each with its own characteristic Emotion.

THE STAR OF DAVID COMPRISES TWO OVERLAPPING TRIANGLES

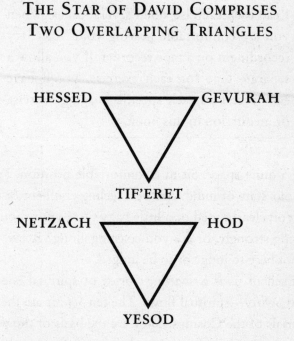

The Kabbalah alludes to the six points as representing the dimensions of six cubits square of each of the two tablets of the Ten

Commandments. Maimonides maintains that each tablet was a perfect square and that each square was six cubits in length and breadth.

Now we will begin our exploration of how the ten *Sefirot* can guide us in reaching our full potential.

Read each exercise aloud several times. When you are comfortable hearing your voice, try recording it on a tape recorder. If you allow a separate tape for each exercise, you'll have easy access to each specific imaging exercise or meditation in this book.

Find a quiet space. Sit in a comfortable position. Focus on your state of mind. Are you feeling ebullient or sad? Are you clearheaded or a little hazy? Are your thoughts flowing strongly, or are you coasting along? Relax. You are not here to judge or to be judged.

Each of us is a swirling vortex of spiritual energies called *Sefirot*—spiritual flows. The ten *Sefirot* are the raw materials of the Cosmos. They are the basis of the world of time and space, of energy and matter. *Sefirot* are also the building blocks of our individual personalities. Though spiritual in nature, they ultimately become Mind (*Seichel*) and Emotions (*Middot*). The Soul (*Neshama*) is the pathway through which the energy from these sources flow to animate our being. Where do they originate? These ten *Sefirot* flow from the infinite source of *Ein Sof* (literally "Without End") through four parallel spiritual realms.

Ultimately their human manifestations take place in the final realm of *Assiya*. The person you are is determined by the *Sefirot* in the realm of *Assiya*.

Olamot: The Parallel Worlds

The word *Olamot* means "Worlds" in Hebrew. Although our diagram shows four basic realms, in truth the number is infinite. Think of them as dimensions that refract the light of creation. The *Sefirotic* array in the diagram on page 56 can be viewed as a beam of source energy, with ten distinct wavelengths. As these ten waves of creative light pass through the individual realms, their qualities become the "creatures" in that realm, occupying the spiritual "space." They are sometimes perceived as angelic forms, like *serafim* ("angels of fire"), *chayot hakodesh* ("holy animals"), *ophanim* ("wheels"), and angels like Michael, Gabriel, Oriel, and Refael. And there are innumerable others, all influencing activities in the finite physical realm.

The realm of *Atzilut* is closest to the Divine Source. It is indistinguishable from the light of infinity, *Ohr Ein Sof,* (literally "Light of Infinity"). *Ohr Ein Sof* is a

THE SEFIROT & PARALLEL WORLDS

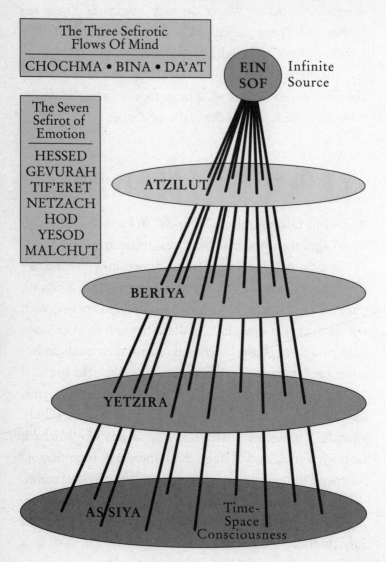

The Three Sefirotic
Flows Of Mind

CHOCHMA • BINA • DA'AT

EIN
SOF

Infinite
Source

The Seven
Sefirot of
Emotion

HESSED
GEVURAH
TIF'ERET
NETZACH
HOD
YESOD
MALCHUT

ATZILUT

BERIYA

YETZIRA

ASSIYA

Time-
Space
Consciousness

THE STAR OF DAVID

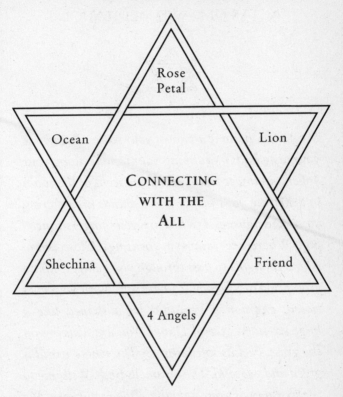

Rose
Petal

Ocean

Lion

CONNECTING
WITH THE
ALL

Shechina

Friend

4 Angels

metaphor for G-d—the light of the One who is Infinite. Little can be said about this Source that is intelligible to our finite minds.

Beriya ("Distinct Creation") is the first realm in which we can discern separate identity, although it is highly spiritualized. *Beriya* is dominated by the innate nature of Mind.

A STAR OF DAVID MEDITATION

Breathe in. Become aware of your senses. Recognize your taste buds by rubbing your tongue along your upper and lower teeth. Allow the scent of the room to penetrate your being. What sounds are entering your consciousness? What are your fingers touching? Where are your eyes focusing? Close them. Allow thoughts to pass through you gently with no prompting or urgency. You are safe. With your eyes closed, envision a beautiful lawn shaped like a huge six-sided Star of David. You are walking on the grass. Feel its soft lushness. The whole world is green and peaceful. The air smells fresh. Welcome to the first day of your new life. Open your eyes. We will revisit this beautiful place that exists for you alone, outside of time. Over time, we will add other images. For now, it is enough to know that it exists and that you can return to it any time you wish.

Yetzira ("Shape and Quality") is the realm of Emotion.

Assiya ("Actualization") is where we dwell. It is the realm of time, space, and earthly consciousness.

Aztilut	The Divine Will
Beriya	The innate nature of Mind
Yetzira	The realm of Emotion
Assiya	Time, space, and earthly consciousness

The *Neshama* (Soul)

Neshama ("soul") is akin to a spiritual umbilical cord that transcends these four realms, one end connected to the Infinite Source and the other located within our spiritual and physical being (see page 36). The *neshama* is the conduit for the flow of the ten *Sefirot,* which then become individuated as ten qualities of personality— our Mind and Emotion flows. The ten *Sefirot* can be divided into two groups.

1. **Seichel** represents the three *Sefirotic* flows of Mind, known as *Chochma, Bina,* and *Da'at.* They express themselves most fully in the realm of *Beriya.*

2. **Middot** represents the seven *Sefirotic* flows of Emotion: *Hessed, Gevurah, Tif'eret, Netzach, Hod, Yesod,* and *Malchut.* They express themselves most fully in the realm of *Yetzira.*

The upper realms of the *Sefirot* are literally unembodied Mind and Emotion.

The embodied soul, the human, is the wild card of creation. In this realm human beings assume consciousness—with the ability to exercise choice.

Each of us draws down a different balance of Mind and Emotion flows in response to our level of wisdom or foolishness.

Seichel: The Three *Sefirotic* Flows of Mind

CHOCHMA: *Chochma* is the spiritual flow that is responsible for inspiration and creativity. The Kabbalah teaches us that *Chochma* is the catalyst that draws out our soul's powers from the deep and uncharted waters of subconsciousness into the light of conscious awareness. Whenever we start to think, the *Sefira* of *Chochma* is the spark that has ignited the process.

Chochma is at work when you realize you are about to solve a thorny problem. *Chochma* literally means

"Wisdom," but it can also be the source of poor "Inspiration" that leads to misinterpretations.

BINA: The initial *Chochma* "spark of thought consciousness" is both shapeless and momentary. It is an "embryo of the Mind" that would be stillborn were it not for the flow of the second *Sefira* of the Mind—*Bina*. *Bina* is feminine in relationship to the masculine *Chochma*. It nurtures the spark of thought consciousness, makes it tangible, and gives it direction. The thought line is now established. Thought becomes analytical, developed, crystallized.

DA'AT: *Chochma* and *Bina* are the cerebral activity of the Mind. Information has been interpreted through *Chochma* and *Bina,* but the emotional climate within has not yet been established. This momentary hiatus before a feeling is established may last only a split second. Or it could be the product of months of struggle, leading to a new flow of Emotions from the same set of thoughts. The *Sefira* of *Da'at* allows the Mind and Emotions to connect. *Da'at* fuses the spiritual energies of Mind to those of Emotion. *Da'at* literally means "Knowing." To really *know* something is to join with it—become one with it. We will also consider another aspect of *Da'at*. It provides the force of attraction between *Chochma* and *Bina,* allowing thought, creativity, and the process of development of thought to merge into a cogent thought sequence.

Middot—The Seven *Sefirotic* Flows of Emotion

We have seven *Sefirot* of Emotion, and they are divided into two groups: internalized emotions and externalized emotions.

INTERNALIZED EMOTIONS

HESSED: When the *Sefirot* become embodied in seven human Emotions they are called *Middot*—which means "Measured Flows." The most basic Emotion, that of giving and sharing, is called *Hessed.* When we reach out to a person in need we are drawing on our *Hessed* flow. It ignites the wish to share both materially and emotionally. It is also the basic Cosmic flow with which creation is imbued.

But *Hessed* is a *feeling,* and innately feelings do not possess direction. Direction is a construct of the Mind, and it is important that the *Hessed* flow be guided wisely. If not, it can become destructive. For example, a generous and giving individual who does not exercise wise restraint runs the risk of running out of steam and resources, becoming emotionally (and even financially) burned out. *Hessed* must be guided by the *Sefirot* of Mind—that is, of wisdom.

GEVURAH: The *Hessed* flow of giving is balanced by the seemingly opposite nature of *Gevurah*. The character of *Gevurah* is to retain, focus, and limit. For example, it restricts the flow of *Hessed* to what is wise in the moment. It should be noted that neither *Hessed* nor *Gevurah* is innately good or bad. The way that our higher Mind exercises choice determines whether the emotion is correctly balanced. Sometimes giving is good. Sometimes withholding is good. Whereas *Hessed* is expansive, spreading out, moving away from self, *Gevurah* is focused, inward oriented, and concentrated.

For example, *Gevurah* is central to the practice of karate, where withholding the dissipation of energy and focusing it in a tight narrow "beam" allows for the concentration of amazing strength. *Hessed,* on the other hand, is essential to the 360 degrees of awareness in which a samurai warrior was trained, or it manifests in the broadness of compassion. Both of these feelings can be intense or weak, depending upon the quantum of flow that is generated.

TIF'ERET: Hessed and *Gevurah* are independent flows. They need to be integrated to achieve balance. The flow of *Tif'eret* facilitates this merger. For example, what happens when we wish to help a friend who is chronically in debt? Our instinct to write a check might be tempered by the knowledge that giving in this instance might actually perpetuate a problem that has been plaguing our friend for some time. We conclude that it might be more helpful if we suggest that the person seek the services of a not-for-profit financial counselor and take control of the situation. Our resolution might be to exercise compassion and give a little more than we intended, while also suggesting a long-term solution. Compassion becomes the integrating force for *Hessed* and *Gevurah*. The function of *Tif'eret* is to organize the combination once the Mind has determined how the feelings should be blended.

These three *Sefirot* of Emotion are the internalized feelings. They are experienced within, before their expression in the real world. To *externalize* them, another set of three *Sefirotic* flows has to be initiated. Without them, feelings would forever be emoted, but no relationships would result because of the lack of reaching out.

EXTERNALIZED EMOTIONS

NETZACH: Once the inner emotional climate becomes established, the Emotions seek actualization through relationships. The first of these expressive flows is that of *Netzach.* This flow is the *Sefira* responsible for the urge to reach out into another person's world. It may mean entering into conversation, or extending a hand, or performing actions that touch another in myriad ways. *Netzach* allows us to cross the interpersonal boundary. *Netzach* literally means "Victory"—the success of crossing the threshold of self and stepping into the other's space.

HOD: Successful relationships are not solely the result of reaching out. They also depend upon our ability to create the inner space to accept the *Netzach* flow extended by others. If we extend ourselves to another with great enthusiasm and find the emotional climate chilling, we have not created a relationship.

The flow of *Hod* holds back the thrust of *Netzach* so that we do not become dominating or overly effusive and create fear or emotional suffocation. The way that *Hod* restrains *Netzach* in the world of expression is not unlike the way that *Gevurah* impinges upon *Hessed* in the world of internal emotions.

YESOD: The essence of *Yesod* is our ability to focus on the person with whom we are communicating. It is the funnel through which all the *Sefirot* of Mind and Emotion pour into a relationship. The word *Yesod* literally means "Foundation," and the Kabbalah teaches us that *Yesod* denotes the intensity, bonding, and strength of communication that exist between two people.

MALCHUT: Just as a corner defines the meeting of two or more lines, so *Malchut* becomes the meeting point of all the *Sefirotic* flows—their final expression. But just as a corner is nothing without the lines that create it, *Malchut* is the juncture at which the "lines" of the Mind-based *Sefirot* and the Emotion-based *Sefirot* intersect. It represents the final cohesion in a relationship. It is the fertile ground in which the *Sefirot* are planted and the pinnacle of femininity among the *Sefirot*.

The three tools, *Chochma, Bina,* and *Da'at,* are basic to mastering the processes of Mind. We will now isolate them and focus on each in turn, learning how they operate.

5

Chochma:
The Magician's Wand

How do you trace a thought back to its subconscious origins? How do you create a more positive flow from the same subconscious catalyst? The Mind does not record objectively. It interprets, and it always possesses a bias. In fact, all consciousness possesses a bias. From the range of possible interpretations, we need to train our *Chochma* to draw positive and benevolent interpretations from our subconscious.

For example, the flower growing in a garden bed is not merely a collection of molecules configured in a complex manner and subject to description by mathematical and chemical formulas. The delicate flower that basks in the warmth of the sun is a play of light and shadow. It evokes feelings and memories. It can transcend time and propel us back to our childhood. It can fill our mind with the vision of a loved one. It can rivet us with awe at its breathtaking beauty. Yet this interpretation is rare. Most people go through life with their inspirations stillborn. Wouldn't it be wonderful to cultivate a creativity climate that would inspire us with this magic?

The *Sefira* of *Chochma* can act like a magician's wand. It allows us to conjure a thought and imbue it with the multicolors of awareness.

> You are where your thoughts are.
> —HASSIDIC MASTER

Gone Fishing for Your Thoughts

Think of yourself as a deep pond fed by the gushing waterfall of the *Sefirot*. You are also the one who fishes in that pond. Your natural disposition can be likened to a fishing reel. Your deeper wants and wishes are the bait. The way you pursue joy and alleviate pain is represented by the area of the lake where you prefer to fish. Your thoughts are the fish you catch. Most of us fish in exactly the same way, in exactly the same area of the pond, and we always catch the same fish. In general, we respond in the same way to the same stimuli.

If we persist in interpreting an event in the same negative way—hurtful and fear laden—then our brain will persist in delivering its characteristic load of excessive stress, releasing hormones that trigger a chain reaction of biochemical events.

Scientists have verified that the body's memory of fear is the emotion most deeply recorded in the brain's memory banks. For instance, if you remember a traumatic job interview at which the interviewer tried to discredit and demean you, that memory will become part of the recorded information your brain relays to your body every time you enter an interview room. Just thinking about it, you may find that your palms grow sweaty, your face flushes with discomfort, and your heart beats uncomfortably loud in your chest.

Is it possible to reinterpret consciously negative circumstances as positive outcomes? Might living in denial invite its own dangers? The truth is that very little in life is categorically positive or negative. Most of the circumstances we face, even the seemingly insurmountable obstacles, are the product of subjective interpretations. Can we really know that the business deal we lost might not prove to be a stepping stone to an even better one? Are we in a position to determine whether being spurned by a love interest might not eventually lead to permanent joy and happiness with another? Is it possible that an illness might not prove to be the very trial that strengthens our resolve in another area of our life?

Yet some people consistently get up on the wrong side of the bed, smash their head into the wall of fear and doubt, and stumble anxiously through the day. Others face the same travails and interpret the same reality as an opportunity. Is one of them right and the other wrong? Not empirically, but if the criterion is health and well-being, obviously the latter attitude is miles ahead.

Kabbalah maintains that spiritual repose can be trained and mastered. You can learn how to reinterpret reality. You can draw upon, and maintain, a positive disposition by catching "different fish"—by metaphorically changing your fishing style. You can become a happier and more likable person and also profoundly alter the chemistry of your body. You can obliterate the old grooves of fear and form new tracks, with new interpretations of old memories. Kabbalah even goes one step further. Joy and happiness are the soul's expression of its successful navigation of the sea of the body. The nerve endings, the cell receptors, and the billions of microscopic events right down to the cellular level are the channels for the soul's journey.

A THOUGHT EXERCISE

You will need a digital watch with an alarm or a small alarm clock. You will also need a notebook. At the beginning of a week that isn't too loaded down with appointments, set the alarm for two hourly intervals. Over the course of a week, whenever the alarm goes off, summarize your thoughts in a few words:

- **Describe the thought**—One sentence will do.
- **Origin of the thought**—What triggered it?
- **Value of the thought**—Was it good, useful, hurtful, or angry?
- **Substitute the thought**—If you are unhappy with the thought, how might you have thought otherwise?

You'll be surprised how fascinating this exercise can be, and it takes only a minute or two to jot down your response. Adjust the time intervals when necessary. Obviously if you are in an important meeting, you might not want to take time off to note your thoughts. It is more important to discover your thought patterns over time than to slavishly follow the schedule. At the end of the week study your observations and see if you can detect a trend. How did you react to a stressful situation or unexpected event? Were your thoughts angry? Happy? Disappointed? Hurt? Spiteful? Or did you think things through and work toward a rational and balanced assessment of the events?

This exercise will help you discover your *Chochma* profile—your "automatic pilot setting." By examining how you might have substituted different thoughts, you will gradually learn how to change your setting.

The Megawatt Light Bulb

Imagine a megawatt light bulb. Turn it on and you are blinded by its radiant brightness. Try covering it with a lampshade, but it is far too bright. Another cover: still no good. Keep adding covers until you are comfortable. Only after you have covered the light several times with translucent shades are you able to see. Now, isn't this ironic? In order to open your eyes without pain you have to hide the source of light.

Kabbalists call the *Sefira* of *Chochma mocha setuma*, "the hidden brain." It is a metaphor for the subconscious state. Hassidic *rebbes* rearranged the Hebrew letters of the word *Chochma* to read *koach mah*, meaning "potential." It represents the basic elements of our personality. *Chochma* allows us to draw from the subconscious, and it is also the basic substance of our thoughts and feelings. *Chochma* is the bedrock upon which we build. Cosmically *Chochma* refers to the primordial spiritual inspiration from which the Cosmos evolved. It is the root of the four spiritual elements of fire, water, earth, and air.

The Ephemeral Nature of Chochma

The *Sefira* of *Chochma,* like all the *Sefirot,* is an immensely bright spiritual light. Were its light to remain undimmed, it would be spiritually blinding. No thoughts could come into conscious being. The finite body could not contain such an intense flow of energy. So its brightness is dimmed through "translucent covers" of *Olamot*— the parallel worlds. Once the *Sefira* of *Chochma* has "traveled down here" through the four worlds, it is sufficiently muted to allow us to draw a single spark at a time from the subconscious world within. This spark of consciousness is but a minute facet of our psychospiritual climate.

Yet through the "veiling of the Creator's countenance," as Kabbalah describes this phenomenon, we are given consciousness, a physical world, choice, and even the exercise of poor choice to the extent that evil can exist.

ॐ

At a Kabbalistic level colors are reflections of the basic *Sefirot* of Emotion. There are seven colors of the rainbow, and there are seven *Sefirot* of Emotion. The following exercise utilizes biofeedback to help us learn to monitor the colors of our feelings to better control our Emotion flows. Emotion is a product of Mind interpretation, and by mastering this exercise, we can effectively master the way we draw from the pond of subconsciousness—the *Chochma*.

A *Chochma* Flow Exercise

Breathe in. Become aware of your senses. Recognize your taste buds by rubbing your tongue along your upper and lower teeth. Allow the scent of the room to penetrate your being. What sounds are entering your consciousness? What are your fingers touching? What are your eyes focused on? Now close them. Allow thoughts to pass through you gently with no prompting or urgency. You are safe.

It is very dark. Allow your mind's eye to adjust. It is a quiet, peaceful darkness. You are enveloped in calm. You see a large, shimmering television monitor that does not seem quite solid. It has a fluid quality. Focus on the screen. Stare at its shimmering translucence. Become enveloped in its quiet glow.

Imagine colors that begin to flash outward from the screen. They may frighten you a little at first. But be aware that you have control over the colors. Feel their presence in the room. The first colors are red, orange, and yellow. Look at them flash. They are colors of withdrawal—colors due to fear. Remember: You have control over the colors. Observe them calmly. Watch them become shades of green and then blue. Finally, when you are completely relaxed, they become clear. Meditate on the "no-color."

Think of an event that happened today that left a strong impression on you. Spend a few moments on this event. What color does this event engender in you? Look at the screen. Observe the colors that flow from it into the room. If they are reddish, think back to your event and view it in a detached manner. See it as an objective stranger might. What are the three most distinct features of the event? How did you respond? Was this response appropriate? Could it be handled better? Look at the screen again. You might see the colors transform themselves toward greens and blues. Perhaps they are growing even paler. Become aware of your inner climate. It has become calmer. Reflect on your mind. It has slowed down. The "color" is clear.

Go through this exercise as many times as you need to elicit shades of blue and then clear.

The Inner Duality

From time to time we all catch ourselves thinking, This isn't really me acting like this. It's not like me to be so cranky. Why am I trying so hard to impress? Why am I moping around? What's going on? In that moment of clarity a truer part of ourselves takes hold and brings honesty to our inner vision. Our inner being has taken a look at our outer manifestation. But why can't our "inside" be our "outside"—all the time? Why are we all so oblivious of our truer selves?

Our aim is to learn to use the *Chochma* spark wisely. If the spark is drawn from wisdom, it burns truly. If, however, we allow ego and insecurity to tap into *Chochma,* then the fire it creates is fed by a false image of ourselves. This inner duality of ego and selflessness is called in *Hassidic* terms *Nefesh Behamit* and *Nefesh Elokit.* These terms translate to mean the "Animalistic Soul" and the "G-dly Soul"—the source of challenge and inner conflict.

The nature of human motivation has everything to do with the quest for becoming one—both within and with each other. We are always facing a fork in the road as we struggle with two competing spiritual inclinations. The first is the quest for physical survival, maintenance, and self-importance. The second is the realization that there is more to life than subsistence and self-glorification—the deeper meaning of relationship.

The *Nefesh Behamit,* the "animalistic" side of the soul, is responsible for the drive for self-preservation. Initially it is the quest for food and shelter. When these needs are satisfied, it becomes a self-perpetuating search for enhanced creature comforts and self-aggrandizement. On the other hand, the *Nefesh Elokit,* the "G-dly" side of our soul, connects us to higher aspirations and unity with another soul.

The competing interests of these two tendencies come to the fore in the face of a challenge or adversity. For example, it happens when a friend accuses you of insensitivity. You could take offense because the accusation diminishes you in some way. You might want to negate the comment by casting doubt on your friend's motives. Another conceivable response would be to acknowledge the statement and consider how the impression could have arisen and how it might possibly be accurate. The first response is classical *Nefesh Behamit.* The spark of thought, the *Chochma,* drew its strength from your sense of insecurity—a diminution of your worth. In some way the accusation of insensitivity diminished you in your own eyes. The second response draws its strength from the *Nefesh Elokit.* It seeks a true connection to others and uses empathy as its guiding light.

The *Nefesh Behamit* is not all bad. It fuels our drives for self-preservation, and without them we could not engage in higher endeavors. But acting alone, the *Nefesh Behamit* would force us to remain fixated on ourselves long after the basic needs had been met. An internal balance takes place when our physical requirements are satisfied. The *Nefesh Elokit* neutralizes the *Nefesh Behamit* and engages our attention and our higher awareness toward the work of relating.

The *Nefesh Behamit* is self-centered.

The *Nefesh Elokit* is other-centered.

It is from the internal arena of this inner duality that the *Chochma* spark of consciousness arises. If the *Nefesh Behamit* remains in ascendancy, then the spark of thought is colored by ego considerations. The resulting thought sequence and emotion also follow the lead of the ego. The result is disharmony with others and inner fragmentation. The interplay between the *Nefesh Elokit* and *Nefesh Behamit* will occupy our consideration further when we discuss the dynamic of choice and decision making. At this stage it is sufficient to note that *Chochma* does not operate in a vacuum.

Now we can understand that moment when we caught ourselves acting in an uncharacteristic fashion.

אָלֶף   A MEDITATION ON THE LETTER
ALEPH

The numerical value of aleph is one. It represents the eternal G-d. Its energy is timeless and beyond measure. It is the infinite.

ALEPH   *The aleph has three elements: the upper pointer, the lower pointer, and the diagonal connector. The aleph is the letter of personal integration. It teaches us that when we are truly whole both dimensions exist in balance within our being. The diagonal transformer redirects egocentricity into a posture of positive self-worth— recognition of your gifts and uniqueness. The higher-order self directs your behavior so that the gift can be conferred upon others, leading to close-knit relationships, peace, and harmony.*

Look at the upper pointer. The upper pointer refers to your higher-order self called Nefesh Elokit *(the divine component of the soul). Feel yourself inhaling the breath of G-d. Feel your connection to the Divine Presence. Now look at the lower portion. The lower pointer refers to your lower-order self, the* Nefesh Behamit *(the "animalistic" tendency latent in the soul). Once again, inhale the breath of G-d. Meditate for a full minute on how these two strokes coexist within you. Now look at the connecting stroke that balances the two. Meditate on the* Nefesh Elokit *and the* Nefesh Behamit: *the lower-order self representing ego and the higher-order self representing selflessness and humility.*

The first time you approach this meditation you want simply to acknowledge the questions raised. You are not in competition with yourself. You are seeking to understand.

The answers will come in time:

Are your Nefesh Elokit *(G-dly soul) and* Nefesh Behamit *(animalistic soul) in balance?*

How is your Nefesh Behamit *manifest?*

What aspects keep you out of balance?

If you were in perfect synchronicity with the universe, how would you behave?

That inner knowledge was the insight of the *Nefesh Elokit*—the higher-order self. The "misbehavior" was the product of the dominance in the moment of the *Nefesh Behamit.*

It is said that Socrates was once caught by his students in an act unbecoming the great philosopher. His response was said to be, "At this moment I am not Socrates." The challenge of self-mastery is to be our true selves all the time.

Changing *Chochma* changes life. It takes the moment at hand and transforms what might have been formerly interpreted as an adversity into an opportunity—to see the moment through a new lens and a new truth.

6

Bina: Changing Patterns of Thinking

According to widely acclaimed author and doctor Deepak Chopra, we think about one hundred thousand thoughts a day. But about 95 percent of these are repeated day in and day out. Our mind climate seems to be both boring and inflexible. No wonder we feel ourselves replaying the same old record over and over again.

Do you respond the same way each time you are confronted by someone you dislike? Do you feel anger welling up inside you when you think about the occasion you felt humiliated? When budget issues arise do you always become anxious? You often see people repeating the same mistakes at work and at home. Fear and insecurity carve out these grooves of habit. The key to creating change lies in recognizing these habits of the mind. The function of the *Sefira* of *Bina* is to take the creative spark of reinterpretation (*Chochma*) and redirect it into a new way of thinking.

The process of change from fixed responses, repetitive errors, and inflexibility of mind requires our conscious involvement in the transition of *Chochma* thought sparks into the maturity of the *Bina* flow. If *Chochma* is the way we draw on our source for inspiration and creativity of mind, *Bina* is the way that spark of inspiration becomes a cogent thought sequence. *Chochma* "fished" for that thought. *Bina* "cooks" that "fish."

When you learn how to imbue your *Chochma* thought process with *Bina,* the thought becomes analytical, developed, and crystallized and the process of self-refinement even more dramatic. Understanding replaces impatience. Energetic strategies for change replace anger. Instead of struggling to control life, you practice faith and acceptance. The Kabbalah literature calls this accomplishment *re'iyat halev,* "the insight of the heart."

The Cord of Many Colors

It may be useful to further understand the distinction between *Chochma* and *Bina*. Recall that ten spiritual flows express our personalities. They constitute our Mind and Heart. *Chochma* and *Bina* relate to Mind. *Chochma* is creative, and *Bina* is developmental. They are expressions of the soul and are manifest through the labyrinth of the Mind. Even the most subtle of the brain activities, down to the molecular and even subatomic levels, are physiological "clothes" in which the soul "dresses" itself. The process of "dressing" is what we call Mind.

All ten *Sefirotic* spiritual flows interrelate and intertwine. In truth, each *Sefira* has all other nine contained within it. Picture the *Sefirot* as cords with ten strands in each cord, each strand a different color. The individual *Sefira*'s character is determined by the dominance of one of these colors. So were we to attribute the color blue to *Chochma* and yellow to *Bina,* a *Chochma* cord might have a bluish appearance, but with all the other nine colors present as well, while the *Bina* cord would be yellowish, with all the other nine colors present.

Now let me add a further quality to this metaphor. Each colored strand has its own magnetic force, and it attracts the same colored strand in the other *Sefirot*. If we were to throw these ten cords into a bundle, each color would attract its like color in the other *Sefirot*. The

84

resulting shape of this heap of ten cords would depend on how these forces of attraction connected. The shape would depend on how we threw them together.

This is exactly what happens when we think a thought that gives rise to a feeling. The ten *Sefirot* cords "pull" together, resulting in a "shape"—the Mind-Emotion-Behavior attributes in that moment. The "shape" of my response depends on my Mind balance, direction, and the degree of energy I generate to one or more of the Emotions. I might make the blue strand attract all the other blue strands more powerfully than the force of the yellows, resulting in greater inspiration and creativity. Or the yellows might be relating more strongly to the other yellows, causing me to engage in a more cognitive activity.

People are spiritually imbued with specific orientations. Some people by nature are more creatively inclined. They are the world's artists, architects, poets. Others are more technologically inclined, such as engineers, computer software writers, and bricklayers. This is not to say that an artist may not be a clear thinker or bricklayers uncreative. But each of us possesses a certain constellation of inner *Sefirot*ic flows that define our personality. Through the amplitude of attractive force we supply to each strand, we can radically alter the actual outcomes of our Mind-Emotion-Behavior sequence. We can, in fact, consciously intervene by altering the direction and thrust of the *Sefirotic* flows. If we are aware and consistent in a pattern of intervention, it will become part of our refined personality. The correct quantum of *Chochma* (creativity, inspiration, emergence from pre-consciousness) or of *Bina* (developmental, sequenced, ordered, syllogistic reasoning) depends on our discipline and wisdom.

Male and Female

Duality characterizes the Cosmos. Even the human form reflects it. We have two hands, two eyes, two nostrils, and two hemispheres of the brain. There is male and female. The same holds true for the nature of the world. There is an up-down, a right-left, a positive-negative, a proton-electron, a particle-wave, a right-wrong.

Kabbalah reflects this duality by attributing masculine and feminine qualities to all things of existence. Even the *Sefirot* contain masculine and feminine qualities. So, although *Chochma* is masculine compared to the feminine *Bina,* both *Chochma* and *Bina* are masculine vis-à-vis the seven *Sefirot* of Emotion. And the nine *Sefirot,* from *Chochma* through *Yesod,* are masculine relative to the tenth *Sefira* of *Malchut.*

Kabbalah also employs sexual imagery to describe these relationships. The Zohar states that *Chochma* deposits its seed in the womb of *Bina,* impregnating it. This union creates conception, labor, and finally the birth of seven children—the *Sefirot* of Emotion. In this way Kabbalah depicts the character of *Chochma* as male relative to *Bina.* Duality is also reflected in the characteristics of these two *Sefirot.* In the same way that man is perceived as seeking and conquering, so too does *Chochma* "seek" within the subconscious and "conquer" by raising what it "finds" into our consciousness.

Bina, on the other hand, through its feminine nature, nurtures the *Chochma* spark, the seed, until it matures. *Bina* nurtures the point of inspiration and allows it to mature into appropriate expression in the world of consciousness. The seminal idea or "conception" becomes a developed thought sequence.

Without stereotyping the masculine-feminine dichotomy, Kabbalah attributes "nurture" to the feminine nature and "conquering" to the masculine nature. That is not to say that all women are nurturers and all men are "conquerors." Kabbalah also teaches that both men and women have properties of each other—men possessing latent feminine characteristics and vice versa. This duality within both men and women is attributed to the first Person, Adam, who inherently possessed both sets of characteristics. As we read in part 1, Adam was a manwoman composite until the division into Adam and Eve. But the first man and woman each retained characteristics of the other, which is why you and I possess both masculine and feminine traits. A man can utilize his feminine traits when he nurtures his children. Similarly, a mother can express drive and assertiveness in the business world.

Chochma is by nature a seeker and outward directed, while *Bina* is inward directed. *Chochma* is an initiator, and *Bina* is a nurturer. The *Chochma* "thought-fetus" grows in *Bina*'s womb. It matures into a thought flow and is ready to be released from the womb and into a concrete reality of words and actions.

When *Chochma* is not consciously and carefully nurtured in the garden of *Bina*, the wild grasses of ill-directed thoughts and weeds of envy, greed, and ego will flourish. The result is a spiritual wilderness. It leads to uncertainty and, in turn, to egocentric and defensive behavior. A pattern sets in, and the freedom to choose the right path is compromised. Life's meaning is lost, all because the transition from *Chochma* through *Bina* was neither understood nor practiced.

Right and Left Brain Activity

It is interesting to compare *Chochma* and *Bina* with the results of right brain and left brain research. Dr. Elmer Green of the Menninger Clinic at Topeka, Kansas, is a foremost scientist in this arena. He has noted that creativity is associated with right brain activity. The left brain activity must be quieted if we are to encourage creativity to come to the fore. The left brain is the rational cortex, developing logic, rationalizing, deducing, and judging. It is akin to the activity of *Bina.* The right brain tends to "see the whole picture." It draws on an "intuitive" response, providing inspiration and creativity that seems very close to the nature of *Chochma.* In fact, Green developed a biofeedback process of training people to elicit theta waves, a sign that the left brain is relaxed, to allow the less defined processes of the right brain to work on a problem. It is conceivable that similar biofeedback techniques could be used to identify *Chochma* and *Bina* spiritual flows.

Within *Chochma* lies the "soul" of the idea. Hence "right brain" people tend to see a problem in an overview rather than grappling with its individual components. Some scientists and artists employ nonanalytic approaches to solve problems. They walk, or meditate, or daydream, or even "sleep on it." This allows right brain activity to emerge—the infusion of a *Chochma* flow.

Although it has become fashionable to call upon right brain activity as a solution to all problems, the truth is that both hemispheres are necessary for their respective capacities. Even the most creative people need discipline and dedication if they are to produce anything worthwhile. This derives from left brain activity. Using a Kabbalistic point of reference, the sparks of *Chochma* must be harnessed by the shaping quality of *Bina*, which taps the *Chochma* energy and puts it to good use. While *Bina* is discipline and definition oriented, it is nevertheless a pathway to creative freedom. All too often creative geniuses remain undiscovered because they lack the capacity to tap creativity in a meaningful and expressive way. Pablo Picasso mastered the mind-body flow to a point where the cubic shapes and juxtaposition of colors captured a dimension of the subject that would otherwise have remained hidden. For Yehudi Menuhin, celebrated violinist, the inanimate wood and strings became living extensions of his own limbs, heart, and soul. This synthesis of painter and canvas, maestro and instrument, is the result of repetitious and self-disciplined practice. Each of these creative geniuses harnessed the creative spark of *Chochma* and nurtured it through discipline and practice through the *Bina* flow.

Bina and Mind Plasticity

Each of the *Sefirot* utilizes various body parts to manifest the soul's expressions. In fact, the Kabbalistic tradition notes 613 "limbs and sinews" that correspond to the 613 mind-body activities. They in turn correspond to the

Jewish system of *mitzvot* (commandments and laws). The intent is to infuse human experience with the 613 spiritual capacities exhibited through the soul.

The soul employs the brain primarily to distribute its capacities and attributes. Promoting the flow of soul through the brain strengthens the brain's physiological prowess. It exercises the "brain muscles." As with all exercise, these "muscles" of the brain grow, producing greater "brainpower."

Here we come upon an important interface between the spiritual and the physical. It has long been suspected that individuals who regularly exercise their brain actually alter their mind's capacities. It has now been verified through experiments done under the auspices of the National Institute of Mental Health. Drs. Karni and Underleider asked volunteers to carry out repetitive activity. They were brain scanned by way of functional magnetic resonance imaging (MRI), enabling investigators to identify the parts of the brain being used. The investigators discovered that the greater the time spent in "practicing" and rehearsing the activity, the more frequent was the convening of like-minded nerve cells in the brain, the more pronounced and enlarged the neural connections. In other words, the brain capacity seemed to increase. The enhanced flow of *Bina* created actual changes in the brain via these increased neural connections.

There seems to be little doubt that we have the capacity to increase our brainpower. The practice of *Bina* is central to this endeavor, as *Bina* is the spiritual flow that consciously takes thoughts and gives them direction through goals; range through elasticity; and vigor through emotional energy.

The Capacity to Change

We can realize our potential, and even increase it, by allowing the initial spark of creativity to blossom through the flow of *Bina*. The Lubavitcher Rebbe insisted that you and I have the ability to change our very natures. It requires systematic introspection, self-scrutiny, and courage. Humans are the artistic expression of the Divine Artist, but we also enjoy a partnership with G-d in completing the artwork of creation.

Coloring Your Inner Landscape— Spiritual Synesthesia

Scientists see the seven colors of the rainbow as wavelengths. The Kabbalah sees the colors of the rainbow as reflections of the basic seven *Sefirot* of Emotion.

We now have a lot of neurological data available on how the brain "tags" perceptions. A small group of people experience a phenomenon known as synesthesia. These people, estimated to be ten in one million, identify sensations differently from the rest of us. They might describe tastes as being round or yellow or describe sights as loud or pink, and so on. An American neurologist, Dr. Richard E. Cytowic, describes this phenomenon in his book *The Man Who Tasted Shapes: A Bizarre Medical Mystery Offers Revolutionary Insights into Emotions, Reasoning, and Consciousness.*

Research has shown that synesthetes, those who have the ability to perceive their sensations in a cross-referential manner, are actually more consciously aware of their normal brain processes and even of their preconscious processing systems. They can follow the sequence of sorting processes that naturally occur in the brain, whereas most of us become conscious only of the dominant signal that the mind chooses to identify—the sound is heard or the sight is seen, and so forth.

While science is decoding the mind processes, Hassidic psychology has gone ahead and taught us how to make use of the phenomenon. The Torah informs us that thirty-five hundred years ago at Mt. Sinai, several million people experienced a form of group synesthesia. Exodus 20:15 notes that "the people saw the sounds." Hassidic psychology explains that in an elevated state the soul's capabilities flow with extraordinary power through the body, resulting in greater inner awareness. The soul's elevated state in the body produces the mass effect of synesthesia.

We must take advantage of our capacity for change by redirecting our *Bina* flow so that we can experience true creative freedom and personal liberty. The following exercise is designed to help us gain access into our emotional states by synesthetically translating feelings into other senses. You will begin to identify emotions and thoughts as colors and shapes. Unlike feelings or thoughts, which are amorphous and difficult to control, these sensory objects carry no judgment. By consciously altering the shapes and colors, the thoughts and feelings can also be changed.

A *BINA* FLOW EXERCISE

Choose a quiet moment and a comfortable setting. Center. Relax. Gently close your eyes, and focus upon your breath for a few minutes. Let your inner eye slowly scan your body from head to toe—your feet, knees, abdomen, chest, shoulders, neck, face, and head. Focus on your senses one by one. Listen to the sounds around you, identifying each separately. Feel the texture of the material upon which your hands are resting. Move your tongue around your teeth. Detect any scent or odor around you. Now relax further and allow thoughts to enter and exit at will. Allow the flow of inner consciousness to come to the fore. Allow your mind pictures to flow freely. In the most casual way, become aware of their sequence and their possible connection. Now move your focus onto your feelings. Retrace your mind images, but note the feeling each image produces. No need to describe or mentally verbalize. Experience the various feelings. Don't become involved. Just be a visitor.

Allow a thought to emerge. Don't judge. Just observe it. Get comfortable with it. Give the thought a shape. Is it circular or oblong? Does it have corners or is it rounded? Is your thought amorphously shaped? When you have its shape fixed in your mind, give it a color. It doesn't matter what color it is—it's your thought, and it can be any color you want. The important thing is that it be an honest representation. Take your time.

Your thought, manifest as a colored shape, is light as a feather. It is moving slowly through space, just above the ground. Provide some landscape. The landscape will in some way relate to the thought. Allow yourself to be purely intuitive. Keep coming back to the thought. Allow it to travel above a variety of landscapes of forms, colors, and shapes. Don't study the landscape forms. Just allow them to be. When you have completed the journey for that thought, bring the thought back down to earth. Relax.

Now allow a new thought to begin its journey. Repeat the exercise. Just go along with it. Allow the landscape to arise organically, unforced. Go back to the first thought. This time, consciously eliminate some of the landscape and replace it with landscape you think might be more appropriate. You may discover that certain symbols cause discomfort, and you can exchange them for ones with which you feel more comfortable.

Over time, return to the thought. Direct its destination. Become more goal oriented in your journeys. Create landscape settings and shortcuts that make the journey more direct and less distracting.

Each time you complete this exercise, record briefly the journeys, their landscapes, their duration, and your feelings—especially the repetitive symbols. Keep a log of your journeys. Repeat this exercise every day for a week.

As you spend more time and frequency engaging in this exercise you will find yourself becoming more aware of how your thoughts flow, what their hidden goals are, and the energies associated with each. The aim of the exercise is to become increasingly proficient in shaping the direction of your thinking and provide it with flexibility and

בֵּית · MEDITATION ON THE LETTER
BET

ב

BET

Bet *is the second letter of the Hebrew alphabet. Its literal meaning in Hebrew is "house." It is the feminine aspect, as compared to* aleph, *which is male.* Bet *is the first letter of the first word in the Torah—*Bereshit. *(In the beginning...)*

Notice the shape, which is like a house. Meditate on its meaning. Imagine the world is a house.

Notice that one side is open to G-d, and the remaining three are closed. In the same way, knowledge of the beginning is closed to us—it is unknowable. Bet *is the second letter, corresponding to the second day of creation, when G-d divided the waters into two realms. Think about the two realms of consciousness—higher and lower.*

The Hebrew word for "blessing" begins with the letter bet—brachah. *Meditate on how the world is built on the beneficent flow of blessing, despite its many challenges and adversities.*

comfort. For example, you might find that a particular thought always makes you anxious. By sending that thought on its travels and observing the scenery you create, you might find ways of redirecting the thought so that the landscapes become easier to handle.

Mastering *Bina* is a technical skill of the Mind. The exercises on page 94 and below will translate into greater awareness of your thinking processes in the everyday circumstances of life, allowing your thoughts to be more constructive, purposeful, positive, and comfortable.

The next two exercises will show you how to tap your potential for Mind focusing—an important element of the *Bina* flow. Try to practice one of them every day for a week.

VISUALIZATION EXERCISES: BECOMING A GOOD "SPARK NURTURER"

EXERCISE 1.

Sit in a comfortable chair and close your eyes. Take a few deep breaths and visualize someone you love. Starting from the top of the head, systematically focus on each feature, working your way down from the hair, the forehead, to the rest of the face, the neck, shoulders, arms, and hands. Then work your way back up from the hands to your face and the top of your head.

Repeat again. If any feature is unclear or difficult to imagine, go back to the previous feature and when you have it clearly in your mind go on to the next feature.

EXERCISE 2.

Imagine the sun rising above a lake. First, focus on the water as the light changes, then the sun coming up over the horizon, moving slowly to a forty-five-degree angle and up until it is directly overhead. Then take the sun backward until it sinks into the water in a glorious sunset.

True integration of *Chochma* with *Bina* is the work of the *Sefira* of *Da'at,* the third *Sefira* and the one that completes the triad of Mind *Sefirot. Da'at* not only brings about the masculine-feminine union of *Chochma* and *Bina,* allowing them to "fall in love," it also allows the thrust of energy known as Emotion to energize the Mind processes, allowing their translation into active expression.

7

Da'at:
The Believing Mind

Mother Teresa and Joseph Stalin each had strong drives. Mother Teresa saved lives; Stalin murdered millions of innocent people. Obviously it is better for the world when someone's drive is matched by a generous and giving disposition. But a drive is neutral. Human choice imbues it with meaning that is good or evil.

We need drive to project our gifts to the Cosmos. But wisdom ensures that our legacy possesses direction and value. Positive drive needs both the wisdom of the Mind and the power of the Emotions. Only then can our drive be used for worthy goals. Only then is the drive governed by true balance.

This balance of wisdom and feeling is achieved through the *Sefira* of *Da'at*. *Da'at* is the *Sefira* that creates the knowing.

A drive is neutral.
Human choice imbues it with value.

Two Kinds of *Da'at*

In his classical work on Hassidism, the *Tanya,* Rabbi Shneur Zalmen of Liadi notes that there are two aspects of *Da'at*. *Da'at Tachton* creates the bond between Mind and Emotion. *Da'at Elyon* unites *Chochma* and *Bina*.

Have you ever walked into a room and then wondered what you were doing there? For a perplexing moment the *Bina* flow lost its spark—its soul of *Chochma*. It was momentarily absent. However, once you retraced your thought sequence you remembered why you were there. In other words, you reintegrated the *Chochma* and the *Bina*. The *Da'at Elyon* had brought them together again.

In fact, *Da'at Elyon* is superior to either *Chochma* or *Bina* alone. In Kabbalistic teachings this level of *Da'at* draws its strength from the *Sefira* of *Keter*. We will not discuss this *Sefira* here because it is so ephemeral that it has little that can help us achieve a conscious change. It is associated with our highest will, but *Da'at Elyon*, the higher *Da'at*, draws from it and therefore possesses the superior properties of both creativity and understanding and more. The process is dynamic.

Da'at is a spiritual aptitude that flows from the soul. The soul's capacities include intellectual potential, and both creativity and understanding are expressed through the processes of the Mind. *Da'at* gathers the information and refines the Mind-person that we are. When we become conscious of its processes we can actualize our insights and positive virtues on the stage of everyday life.

Now we come to the lower form of *Da'at* known as *Da'at Tachton*. This flow of *Da'at* allows the Mind to be infused with the energy of the Heart. It draws from excitement in learning and joy in discovery. It also broadens, deepens and integrates the knowing with the self. The greater the infusion of Emotion into the Mind, the more integrated the knowing with that which is known, and with the process of knowing.

For example, some children know their multiplication tables so well that the answer tumbles out effortlessly. The information is totally integrated into their being, and they don't even have to think before giving the answer. Other children struggle to find the answer. Yet if we were to ask them for statistics about their favorite baseball teams, they could easily rattle off the number of home runs for several seasons. These children also possess mathematical aptitude. What is the difference between the students who find multiplication easy and those for whom it is an unpleasant chore? It lies in the presence of the *Sefira* of *Da'at*. *Da'at* is the glue that combines the joy of the subject with the thinking that goes into remembering. It unites inspiration (*Chochma*) and understanding (*Bina*) with our emotions (the *Sefirot* of Emotion). Thus children who enjoy the meaning behind numbers can assimilate mathematics, whereas those for whom it is a mechanical chore tend to have difficulty.

When I was a senior in high school, my mathematics teacher taught us that the only way to really know a subject was to write a textbook on it. It sounded like a dreadful chore, but I followed her suggestion and discovered that it really worked. Although I had understood the material before, it was not until I struggled to compose an entire book devoted to the subject that I felt it was really part of my being. I *knew* that math so well, it was as though I had fused with it.

Knowing occurs when we see an advertisement that engages us on an emotional level. We find it funny, exciting, or thought-provoking. We *know* in our gut what the ad is telling us. In the same way, a great book will grab the reader at an emotional level when the words jump the chasm between passive intellectual comprehension and go to the heart. We don't merely understand the book or advertisement. We know that it addresses us in a personal way, and we are moved.

Knowing (*Da'at*) and understanding (*Bina*) are distinct processes. As the great juggler Michael Moschen states in Joan Ames's book, *Mastery—Interviews with 30 Remarkable People:* "When you really apply yourself in a skill or discipline, and you achieve something, it's not separate from who you are."

A Euphemism for Love

The *Tanya* tells us that the Hebrew verb "to know" is also the euphemism for sexual union. Rabbi Shneur Zalmen explains that the union between a man and woman is one of the most profound acts of bonding in creation—taking two and uniting them as one. In fact, when the Torah speaks of the first mating between Adam and Eve the phrase is "and Adam knew Eve."

All "knowing" is a state of intimacy. To *know* something is to bond with it. When you know something deeply it becomes a part of you and you become a part of it. No greater unity exists. Rabbi Shneur Zalmen calls this "a wondrous unity," unparalleled by any other experience. He goes on to apply this state of unity to a oneness with the All—the mystic state of losing one's distinctive self and merging with the experiential state of G-dliness.

In the *Tanya* the concept of *Da'at* is applied to humanity's quest for mystical oneness. However, this equally applies to all areas of learning. *The Tanya* notes that the deeper the insight, the deeper the concomitant feeling. When we know something in a superficial way, we are less likely to become emotionally excited by it. *Da'at* allows the Mind to be invigorated by the Heart. Of course, as we shall see, there are times when the Heart "captures" the Mind and we are unwisely invigorated. The result is what we generally call rationalization. However, the more deeply we understand, the greater our emotional flow, the better grounded we are and the stronger our belief.

Inner Knowing

Belief is an accumulation of information plus an innate disposition that creates an inner knowing. When we say we believe something, we generally mean that we have integrated "knower," "knowing," and "known" to a point where they are inseparable. The "knower," the "knowing," and the "known" become one. We just *know*. The information is "glued" through the higher *Da'at* into the unity of *Chochma* and *Bina. Da'at* becomes infused with the essence of both *Bina* and *Chochma,* making it more powerful than each of them. It is suprarational and therefore not subject to ordinary, rational distraction. At these times we have such a strong inner unity of Mind and Emotion that someone else's Mind alone cannot sway us.

If you had tried to convince a twelfth-century person that the world was round, he would have laughed in your face. His daily experience imprinted upon him a belief that the world was flat. He *knew* it was flat, as did most other law-abiding citizens of the day. It was only when the information changed through the early circumnavigators of the world, and kept being repeated, that the new information could displace the old and in time create a new belief of the nature of the earth. The new information created a more powerful inner knowing or belief.

Today you can ask anybody whether the earth revolves around the sun or vice versa and you will be told that since Copernicus, the information is clear—the sun is at the center of the solar system. Even if you were to explain that since Einstein's theory of relativity proved it is impossible to determine with any certainty, in a system of two or more bodies and motion relative to each other, which one is the focus and fulcrum and which is the "follower," it is likely that person will choose not to understand you. The belief in the centrality of the sun is too strong for the new information of relativity to impinge on it. Beliefs are strong and powerful. In our world it will take more information and more heightened experience to displace the belief in the centrality of the sun.

So we can see that there are two distinct processes in *knowing:*

- The information gathering of the Mind.
- The integration of the information with self through the bonding of Mind and Heart.

While mere information gathering may not affect expression and behavior, a belief can have a profound effect. In fact, belief is a very potent tool that shapes not only our choices, expression, and behavior, but our very health and well-being.

The Power of Belief

In his book, *Timeless Healing: The Power and Biology of Belief,* Dr. Herbert Benson points out that for a long time the standard medical treatment for angina included injections of cobra venom or the removal of the thyroid or parts of the pancreas. While we have no reason to believe that any of these remedies should have worked, we do know that, against scientific logic, they had a 70 to 90 percent success rate. Interestingly, when the medical profession began to doubt the value of these treatments, their effectiveness dropped by 30 to 40 percent. In other words, the power of the placebo effect proved twice as effective "under conditions of heightened expectation."

In 1950 Dr. Stewart Wolf studied women who suffered persistent nausea and vomiting during pregnancy. The women were given a substance that induces vomiting, syrup of ipecac, but they were told the medicine would cure their problem. Amazingly, it did.

A 1995 study published in the *Annals of Internal Medicine* showed that patients with rheumatoid arthritis experienced a 50 percent decrease in swelling simply by relying on placebos. Other studies show that mock ultrasound treatments in dentistry reduce pain and produce 30 percent less swelling, and that symptoms of asthma, herpes simplex, duodenal ulcers, and a host of other conditions have been relieved by placebo treatments.

The way information is conveyed to patients has a substantial effect on their recovery. In one recognized British medical journal, Dr. K. B. Thomas wrote that 64 percent of patients who got "good news" were cured within two weeks of consultation, compared with 39 percent who received negative feedback. People who were given the information in a neutral fashion had a 53 percent recovery rate.

I am reminded of Australian aborigines, who punish their worst criminals by a tribal ritual called "pointing of the bone." Administered by a tribal elder, pointing a bone at the accused leads to almost immediate death. Some doctors also tend to "point the bone."

A host of other reported medical studies demonstrate the amazing power that belief has on the function of the body:

- Women who believe they are pregnant will frequently experience pseudopregnancy symptoms.
- Cholesterol-lowering placebos changed the health of a group of men who had suffered heart attacks.
- Taste, color, and number of capsules affect the success of a given treatment.
- Placebos may have the ability to lower the subjective experience of pain.
- Deafness can be self-induced in the wake of tragedy associated with noise, as was discovered in Kobe, Japan, after the earthquake of 1995.

These examples contradict the old Cartesian separation of mind and body. Descartes's conclusion that the two have independent "wiring" has certainly been laid to rest as we recognize the power of the mind to shape the body's functions.

A Consciousness Exercise

Repeat the following exercise daily for a couple of minutes. Find a quiet place. Disconnect the phone.

Ask yourself, What do I know? And what do I *really* know?

Do I know how to fly? Do I know what it is like to swim? Do I know what it is like to smile? Do I know what it is like to breathe?

Of course you do. But do you really know?

Take breathing. What do you know about it? Do you know the air going in? The air passing through your trachea to your lungs? Do you know the consciousness that results from breathing? Do you know the unconsciousness that results from nonbreathing? Do you know the cosmic breath that keeps the Cosmos alive? Do you know who breathes that breath? Do you breathe in rhythm with the breath of life?

Now ask yourself again: What do I know? What do I really *know*?

Live more deeply. Allow the *Da'at* flow to do the connecting, the bonding, the knowing.

The inner knowing and belief of the *Sefira* of *Da'at* becomes a powerful tool with which to expand the

גִּמֶל

A MEDITATION ON THE LETTER
GIMMEL

ג

GIMMEL

Gimmel *is the third letter of the alphabet, and it contains a numeric value of three. Just as* Da'at *stabilizes and balances* Chochma *and* Bina, *so* Gimmel *provides the "third leg" for the letters that precede it. Look at the base of Gimmel and how it provides a firm foundation for a delicate stem. Meditate on Gimmel's essential nature as the bridge between the individual and the home. Its very name is a derivative of the Aramaic word* gamia, *which means "bridge."*

mind as well as to achieve good health and well-being. Through Kabbalah we learn how we can use our power of belief to change not only our body chemistry, but, even more significant, the spiritual wiring of our higher selves. By mastering the *Sefirot* of *Da'at*, we can develop new ways of interpreting the nature of reality. We can learn to balance our mind-body—and achieve good health as well.

Da'at is a spiritual aptitude that flows from the soul. The soul's capacities include intellectual potentials. These become expressed through the physiology of the brain, through the processes of the Mind. The *Da'at* process gathers information and keeps refining the kind of Mind-person that we are. If we can become conscious of its processes, then we will accelerate our self-awareness and allow our personal insight and positive virtues to become actualized in the arena of everyday life.

Through our analysis of *Chochma, Bina,* and *Da'at* we have come to an understanding of what is going on in the head. Now let us turn to an understanding of what happens in the heart. How do you learn to modulate emotions? Indeed, what are emotions? The "flow of feeling" is the subject of the next section.

8

Hessed: Unlocking the Flow of Love

Mind and Emotion

Mind and Emotion are the pathways through which we touch the Cosmos. While words are the vehicles of the Mind's expression, they do not express the flow of Emotion as easily. That's why I can't accurately *tell* you how I *feel.* I can only use metaphors and analogies to convey my feelings. While thoughts provide a framework that makes the universe intelligible, feelings express the amplitude, frequency, and depth of our relationship with the spiritual and physical environment. Feelings do not "talk" to us—they emote within us. They provide us with a framework within which we experience our reality.

Both words and feelings are expressions of the soul. When we touch the Cosmos through Emotion we are connecting in a personal way. No one else tastes the pleasures and pains of life in exactly the same way as you. Our feelings are completely our own. Our individual uniqueness guarantees that each of us reads life differently. That is why it is so exciting to find someone whose experience resonates with our own. It is unusual, and it indicates that we are close in ways that are spiritual.

- MIND is the way the SOUL expresses itself through the physiology of the BRAIN.
- EMOTION is the way the SOUL expresses itself through the metaphoric HEART.

What do we mean by the "metaphoric Heart," and why has the soul a need to express itself anyway?

The Nature of Emotions

Think of the soul as the spiritual umbilical cord that channels natural creative forces of the Cosmos through each one of us. Now think of the physical body as the

COSMOS & PERSON

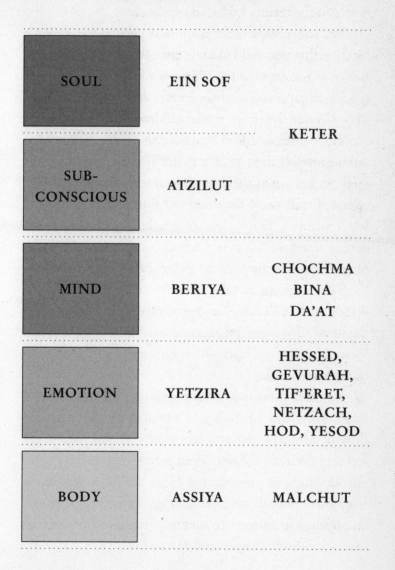

SOUL	EIN SOF	
		KETER
SUB-CONSCIOUS	ATZILUT	
MIND	BERIYA	CHOCHMA BINA DA'AT
EMOTION	YETZIRA	HESSED, GEVURAH, TIF'ERET, NETZACH, HOD, YESOD
BODY	ASSIYA	MALCHUT

"container" and conduit for the expression of those forces in the realm of time and space.

The soul possesses the spiritual capacities for communication that you and I use when we think, speak, and act. But only through the intermediary of the body are these capacities expressed. Latent within these three processes of expression lies the potential of Mind and Emotion.

The conscious Mind expresses the soul's capacity for intelligence. It does so through a specific physiological medium known as the brain. No matter how exquisitely complex and subtle the design of the brain, it nevertheless remains a finite piece of machinery, down to the energy transfers that take place. Its functions can even be observed under the microscope or through scanners.

The working of our Emotion is much harder to detect. It doesn't have a conveniently located organ like the brain. It is a general expression of the soul and is not located in any one place—though we call its "place" the metaphoric Heart.

Emotion is diffused throughout the body. It reflects a generalized flow of the soul compared to the particular flow of Mind. When you feel happy or sad, you don't feel it in your big toe or in your teeth—you feel it generally throughout your being. Here we are referring to emotions rather than tactile feelings. Being more diffuse, emotions are harder to define, pinpoint, or change through conscious intervention.

The Science of Emotion

Although we have a good idea about how the soul is manifest through the brain, the way that the soul is manifest through Emotion defies easy definition. The science of Emotion is just emerging. In recent years science has begun to delve more deeply into the interplay that exists among the Mind, Emotions, and the body. It is interesting to note that the decentralized nature of Emotions that Hassidic psychology describes correlates well with modern research.

Professor Candace Pert is one of the leading researchers in the field of the physiological nature of Emotion. In her book *Molecules of Emotion: Why You Feel the Way You Feel,* she provides a scientific basis for the physiology of Emotion and why it is diffused throughout the body. You may already be familiar with the model of the brain's "communication system" as a giant network of trillions of miles of "wiring" of the central nervous system. Without contradicting this model, she enhances it by hypothesizing a chemical model of ligands and receptors, with each cell having a huge range of receptors with "chemically designed invitations" on their surface. She suggests we think of them as "chemical billboards" that attract protein-laden traveling "chemical clients"—the ligands. Each receptor attracts its particular client. This cellular communication takes place across the endocrine, neurological, gastrointestinal, and immune systems. In other words, each cell "talks" to the body as a whole through a chemical language. It is even said that each cell possesses a "mind" of the whole being.

Interestingly, the area of the brain that we believe to contain most functions of Emotion, the limbic system, contains 95 percent of the neuropeptide receptors. So Emotions are the product not only of electrical stimulation, but of chemical stimulation as well.

Mind and Emotions can be thought of as the flow of information as it moves among the cells. It is now believed that every cell in the body remembers and that these memories are stored throughout the body. In short, the body remembers past feelings! When we experience a feeling we have had before, a neuronal circuit is activated. It generates a total body response, bringing into play a characteristic set of body changes, even including signature facial expressions. A mere shift in thought can induce such a change.

An interesting experiment was recently reported in the *British Psychological Society Journal,* noting that merely thinking about exercise actually increases muscle strength. The implications for recovery from muscle injuries are enormous and may generally enhance performance as well.

While the brain keeps us from being bombarded by sensory stimuli by filtering what we consciously experience, our body as a whole continues to respond subconsciously to the subtleties of unfiltered Emotions. Therefore conscious intervention through meditation can redirect the body's responses. For example, if an individual's deep-seated anger is causing stress that affects the immune system, dealing with the anger can unstress the body and prevent its staying "stuck" in a physiological groove.

Dr. Margaret Kemeny of the University of California did a study of Method actors. She discovered that when an actor simulated sadness, it increased the number of "killer" cells that hunt down cellular abnormalities in his body.

Chiropractic calls this overall body consciousness "innate intelligence," and others call it "the wisdom of the body." Kabbalah calls it the "unified expression of the soul." Kabbalah explains that when you do a *mitzvah* (a good deed), it is a Mind-Emotion-Body behavior that by definition creates an optimal pathway for the soul's expression. Not only do we become more infused with Cosmic flow, but we actually improve the existing Cosmos. Even more specifically, our acts of goodness can tap into diffused Emotions and reorient them so that the result is wellness and good health.

When we do a mitzvah we play a part in completing the unfinished act of creation.

Looking at it from another point of view—that of spiritual growth—we can extrapolate that our feelings can physically alter the body's pathways through which our spiritual flows gain expression. In fact, we are a "seething cauldron" of spiritual *Sefirotic* flows that are influenced by the body's conscious and unconscious processes. The way we choose to interpret the moment (Mind) sets in motion a set of feelings (Emotion), which may result in damage to the body, or its repair and well-being.

Your Giving Nature

Hessed is the emotion of giving and sharing. When we reach out to a person in need, we are drawing on our *Hessed* flow. It is the basic cosmic flow with which creation is imbued. Indeed, we can say that the *Sefira* of *Hessed* is at the heart of humanity's desire to make a meaningful contribution to the world. In Kabbalah, *Hessed* is described through the metaphor of water. Just as water flows downward from higher ground, *Hessed* flows down from the union of *Chochma* and *Bina* through the act of *Da'at*. Like water, *Hessed* is associated with purity and pleasure. We bathe and are made clean. We drink water and are refreshed.

Underlying all spiritual happiness lies a quality of giving, contribution, and service. That is why many spiritual paths have as a central tenet of their teaching the concept of service.

Rabbi Yitzhak of Troyes (known by the acronym Rashi) notes that *Hessed* underlies G-d's motivation to create the world. Kabbalah teaches that the human being is a microcosm of the universe. Even when we don't realize it consciously, each of us is motivated to contribute to the betterment of the world. This is central to the nature of Creation and our own human nature.

Often we have learned behaviors that stymie a healthy *Hessed* flow. I have three friends I will call David, Sara, and Greg. Each of them approaches life in a different way.

DAVID

David lives his life in "fast forward." Life is too short, and there doesn't seem to be enough of anything. He must press on, beating deadlines, surpassing personal goals, and acquiring more physical manifestations of personal worth. He doesn't allow time for committed relationships to develop. Consequently his *Hessed* flow is repressed.

SARA

Sara often colors the present moment with the tones of her past experiences. She loses the freshness of the "now" by constantly reliving lost moments. Sara suffers from bouts of guilt, waking up to the repetitive tune of "what if." What is happening to her *Hessed* flow? It has been redirected through the prism of the ego. *Hessed* is flowing, but it is trapped. Sara needs to develop interests that take her out of herself.

GREG

We have already discussed how David represses his *Hessed* flow and Sara traps hers. Greg, on the other hand, has weakened his *Hessed* flow by directing it solely to large social issues. He volunteers for an international nonprofit agency, because he is committed to social justice. While this is a laudable goal, he has so depleted his *Hessed* flow that he is suffering from burnout.

It is clear that each of my friends needs to redirect the *Hessed* flow so that it will nourish them. When we share our *Hessed* flow with another, whether it be a relative, friend, or member of the community, we are reestablishing the proper balance of energies.

For example, David could benefit from the intimacy of marriage. The compromises and give and take of a long-term, stable relationship would express his *Hessed* energy.

Sara, on the other hand, needs to go out into the world and give to others without involving her ego. She would benefit from doing volunteer work with people whose needs are immediate. Giving her time and attention to a terminally ill person in a hospice or a woman in a shelter would enable her to release her *Hessed.*

Greg should take time off from his volunteer activities and enjoy his friends and family. For example, if he committed to baby-sitting his favorite nephew one evening a week, he would discover the joys of focused *Hessed* flow.

Because I care about my friends, I try to influence them to change their lives. But I have to beware imposing myself on them, even for their own benefit. In other words, I must manage my own *Hessed* flow.

> The negation of ego is what distinguishes
> between the desire to control and dominate
> and the genuine flow of *Hessed.*

A genuine *Hessed* flow is always "other-centered," never self-centered, and this includes giving advice to our friends and family. One way we can test ourselves is to ask, "What do I really care about at this very moment: my battered pride because my advice wasn't accepted or the welfare of my friend?"

> A genuine *Hessed* flow
> evokes the same in others.

The Kabbalah teaches us to identify the *Hessed* flow by sharing ourselves with others through a natural process of self-revelation. Yet we are afraid of revealing ourselves. What do we fear? Pain, rejection, and humiliation.

We must remember that the Creator revealed Itself in the process of creation. The spiritual flow of *Hessed* is the basic undercurrent of creation. In other words, G-d was not withholding when It created the universe, and consequently *our* primary drive is to connect and relate. When we touch the world through verbal contact, through our ability to see and hear, and through our capacity for physical touch, we are manifesting our natural *Hessed* flow. It seems that all aspects of our lives are examples of the potential for spiritual connection.

Hessed is the dominant flow that propels us to a state of oneness and unity. Loneliness is a heavy price to pay for holding back on our natural quality of *Hessed*.

What my three friends sought most of all was the joy of connection. When they come to understand the nature of the *Hessed* flow, their obvious assets and gifts can create bonding and connection. They have within their grasp the means for creating personal fulfillment and closeness with others.

A *HESSED* EXERCISE

Before you begin this exercise, familiarize yourself with the illustration presented here.

THE *CREATOR'S* LOVE

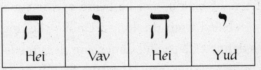

ה	ו	ה	י
Hei	Vav	Hei	Yud

Sit in a comfortable chair. Close your eyes and become calm. You are safe. Open the door to a room with low lighting. Feel a multitude of emotions together in one space. Don't try to understand how feelings can be housed in a room. Just become comfortable with the sensation and move about. Feel the emotion of love. Take a few steps and feel it give way to an intense focused holding in of feelings. Allow yourself to experience whatever feeling you encounter as you walk.

As you move toward the right wall of the room, note how your feelings become giving, loving, contributing, sharing, and servicing. Stay on this side of the room. This is the side of *Hessed.*

Look at the right wall. It is piercing clear white in color. In fact, it is hard to describe the color because it is watery clear. Yet it is opaque. You can't see through it. Stare hard at the wall and you will make out the Hebrew lettering denoting the four-letter name of G-d, the name that stands for the Creator's love and self-revelation. The shapes of the letters suggest a sequence. The first letter, the small "dot," as it is called, the *yud,* is the internal, inscrutable Divine Will. It is the soul that exists in every Hebrew letter. The second letter, the *hei,* the letter of breath, can be heard as the sound of air being exhaled from the lungs. Unlike the dot, it possesses defined shape and dimension. It is the letter that gives existence its form. It is the breath of existence. The third letter is the *vav.* Shaped like a hook, it allows us to hook into the inscrutable Divine Will and gain direction. It allows the flow of creation to flow downward into the realm of dimension, spiritual shape, the spiritual parallel for the physical, finite world. It acts as a funnel for the Divine Will. The final letter is again the letter *hei.* This time it depicts the dimensioned physical world. It represents the energy that maintains the integrity of all physical states.

Focus on the word and the four letters. Experience a profound love and desire to give and share as you move close to this wall. Allow the sequence of the letters to direct your giving flow. Note the source of your love. It may be an abstract inner sense. Experience the source deep within. Focus on it—your *yud.* Now focus on your *hei.* Allow your love and giving to become discernible. Ask yourself how your love feels. Think about how you express unconditional giving. Think about how wonderful it feels to have someone or something with whom to share your giving nature. Now focus on the *vav*—hook the flow on a person, someone you love, by bringing that person into clear focus and seeing your giving nature surround that person. Finally, focus on the *hei* again. This time create imageries of how you can tangibly express your giving nature in the real world. How can you actualize your love? What are the actions and verbal ways you can express your love? See yourself putting these into practice and seeing the responsiveness of the other. Move slowly away from the right wall. Feel the overwhelming power of your love begin to lessen in intensity. Remove your focus from the letters on the wall and allow them to recede into the clear whiteness of the wall.

Become aware of yourself by moving your hands and feet. Come back into this world.

The world has a heart. Feelings flow from the cosmic heart and become the feelings that you and I experience in the mundane world. The Creator used the attribute of *Hessed* as the prime "tool" in the process of creation. So the most normal approach we can take to life is to be giving individuals. When we facilitate the flow of *Hessed*, we align ourselves with the heart of the Cosmos.

David's, Sara's, and Greg's *Hessed* flows are not in alignment with that of the Cosmos. Yet all three have the capacity to rectify their emotional "registry." We all do.

A STAR OF DAVID MEDITATION

Breathe in. Become aware of your senses. Recognize your taste buds by rubbing your tongue along your upper and lower teeth. Allow the scent of the room to penetrate your being. What sounds are entering your consciousness? What are your fingers touching? Where are your eyes focusing? Close them. Allow thoughts to pass through you gently with no prompting or urgency. You are safe. With your eyes closed, envision a beautiful lawn shaped like a huge six-sided Star of David. You are walking on the grass. Feel its soft lushness. Find yourself walking on a jetty looking at the deep blue sea. Identify with the ocean's bold, even heaving as it breathes its ponderous waves. Take time to feel its immense depth and strength. Identify with that strength of purpose. Spend some time contemplating the image of the sea. Breathe its fresh, pure, strong essence.

But we need to discover a pathway, a teacher to assist us. I hope that in reading this book, you will find that pathway.

The Kabbalah teaches that through the act of giving, the giver and the receiver are joined. Hands touch and hearts join.

Hessed and *Gevurah* are the keys to emotional self-awareness.

Abraham as a Paradigm of *Hessed*

The first Hebrew, Abraham, was an enormously giving and loving individual. He expressed his love for G-d by defying the leaders and community of no less a region than Mesopotamia. He waged war against a much stronger army to save his nephew Lot, who, the Bible tells us, was not deserving of his love. He established a tent city in the desert that was renowned for its hospitality. Desert wayfarers knew they were welcome; we are told that Abraham derived great pleasure from sharing his home with strangers and lavishing upon them his largesse. All he asked in return was that they acknowledge that the source of this goodness was the giving Cosmos—a beneficent Creator.

Three days after Abraham was circumcised, he stood outside his tent and searched the horizon for visitors. The day was extremely hot, and travelers stayed indoors to avoid the noonday sun that created a veritable oven of the desert. Yet, notwithstanding the heat and his considerable physical pain, Abraham was disconsolate because he had no guests with whom to share his bounty. He stared at the horizon, as though willing his guests to arrive. G-d took pity on him and sent down angels disguised as desert travelers. Abraham fed them and was comforted.

Abraham's great strength was his loving heart, which

הֵא

A MEDITATION ON THE LETTER
HEI

ה

HEI

G-d's most profound act of giving was breathing life into the nostrils of the creatures It created.

The letter hei signifies breath. Say the letter softly. The sound you hear is that of breath. Meditate on the sound. Think of the profound beauty that exists within the simple act of drawing breath.

Now look at the small gap on the upper left-hand side of the letter. It represents the space through which G-d's light can enter, no matter how dark life may seem. Meditate on the Creator's light reaching into the dark places within.

sought expression in acts of kindness. Therefore his greatest test was when G-d asked him to sacrifice that which he held closest to his heart—his beloved son Isaac. We know that the sacrifice did not take place; G-d sent an angel to stay his hand at the final moment.

It was a test, but it tells us a great deal about Abraham's discipline and self-mastery. He obeyed G-d's command, although it went against his own bountiful *Hessed* flow.

Our biblical forefathers and foremothers were not above human emotions. The point is not that they were perfect. Far from it. They struggled with their emotions, came to understand their weaknesses and to rise above them when G-d commanded.

The Hebrew forefathers Abraham, Isaac, and Jacob personify the inner Emotions of *Hessed, Gevurah,* and *Tif eret.*

A genuine *Hessed* flow is other-centered, never self-centered. However, without the ability to balance a giving nature with wise self-restraint, the capacity to give can run dry or become distorted. The *Sefira* of *Gevurah* is *Hessed*'s counterpoint—and the subject of the next chapter.

9

Gevurah: Drawing
on Inner Strength

Strength takes many forms. Some of us are physically strong, or our strength may lie in our willpower.
We may be strong-minded, or we may allow our feelings
to flow strongly. Perhaps we have strong convictions.
Our faith may be unshakable. The Kabbalah tells us that
each of these forms of strength is connected by a common flow—the flow of *Gevurah.* When we lift a load of
groceries from the trunk of a car, the mind focuses and
the muscles tighten. But beyond the engagement of
mind and body lies the capacity to harness our inner

132

resources. This is the domain of *Gevurah,* the counter-point to *Hessed.*

The *Sefira* of *Gevurah* directs spiritual energy into a defined shape so it can achieve a goal. It harnesses and shapes dispersed energy into sharp relief. Its properties include concentration, discipline, and focus.

Concentration limits the flow of ideas. For example, good teachers limit the flow of information so that it matches the capacity of their students. *Gevurah* harnesses a teacher's natural tendency to give and share and matches it with a student's capacity to understand and absorb. When we restrain ourselves so others have the opportunity to express themselves, we are utilizing our *Gevurah* flow. At these times we screen the information or restrain its flow altogether. Flow screens out extraneous input and creates the narrow channel through which inner strength can flow, and discipline temporarily limits the spread of activity.

We have all seen Mind-directed strength. When a mother suddenly finds that she has the strength to lift a car that is pinning her child beneath its wheels or a soldier carries his wounded buddy for many miles, only to discover much later that he himself has been badly injured; when a karate expert breaks a solid brick with a single blow of his hand or an unseeded tennis player defeats the reigning champion yet remembers little of the event afterwards—we are seeing the flow of *Gevurah* in action.

Hiding in Order to Reveal

The Kabbalah describes the *Sefira* of *Gevurah* as a screen that masks higher reality: In the beginning, the Creator contracted Itself into No Space to allow space for the creation. We call this process *tzimtzum*, which means "self-contraction" or "concealment." In its mystical sense it refers to the process of the Creator limiting and contracting so that existence could come into being. This contraction is known as "the original *Tzimtzum*." Nonetheless, a small degree of creative light filtered through the veil, and the Creator took this blinding light, called *kav*, and sent it through another level of screening known as "minor *tzimtzum*," until only a tiny beam of light could be seen. From this light the Creator fashioned a finite creation. These processes of *tzimtzum* were the original and cosmic expression of the divine *Gevurah*.

In the same way that G-d held back all but the faintest glimmer of creative energy so that finite creation could exist, so too masking information in an analogy or metaphor can, ironically, reveal its essence. It allows the kernel of the concept to sneak through. The cosmic *tzimtzum* did the same. Had G-d filled all space and time, the universe could not have come into being. It was necessary for the Creator to conceal Itself into a spiritual No Space. Likewise, when the *Gevurah* flow holds back an excess of information, it enables the *Hessed* flow of giving to be appropriate—in a form that can be accepted.

Without the balance of *Hessed, Gevurah* can be negative and hurtful. It can be the basis of stinginess, egotism, fear, and emotional withholding. If we are fearful, our *Gevurah* can be hurtful. Hurt and pain early in life can stunt the flow of *Hessed.* In its place the insecure ego adopts a grasping posture—taking rather than giving, holding back rather than sharing. Even the "giving" becomes "taking"—a manipulative strategy. Such people live in constant fear. Their *Gevurah* flows through the lower-order self—the *Nefesh Behamit*; however, in the service of the higher-order self, the *Nefesh Elokit*, it is an appropriate counterpoint to the unmitigated flow of *Hessed.*

As with all our behavior, balance is the key.

Balance of *Hessed* and *Gevurah*

Our natural tendency is to be *Hessed* oriented, but sometimes it is necessary to be highly focused, single-minded, and self-contained to achieve a specific goal. At such times the balance must weigh heavily in favor of *Gevurah* rather than *Hessed.*

Successful people know how to pace themselves. They know that too much, too often, can result in burnout. They know that success does not mean speed. It means holding back when it is appropriate and increasing the pace when it is most needed. Their *Gevurah* and *Hessed* are in harmony. The skills of balance are central to emotional self-mastery. The *Sefira* of *Hessed*, our giving self, must be balanced and tempered by a capacity to contain its flow. Allowing our feelings to flow unchecked will drain them; holding them back constantly is unhealthy and unnatural. *Hessed* must be balanced by *Gevurah,* and *Gevurah* must be freed up through *Hessed.* We must pace our flow of emotions.

Gevurah, Discipline, and the Obstacle of Ego

The *Sefira* of *Gevurah* is the source of discipline of mind and body, involving self-containment, self-control, and self-mastery. The goal is a truer freedom of expression. Janos Starker, a preeminent musician of the twentieth century, attributes his mastery to discipline and self-control. "You have to discipline yourself to learn, study, and practice, practice, practice," he notes in Joan Ames's book, *Mastery—Interviews with 30 Remarkable People.*

How can we distinguish between a mastery that stems from humility—a healthy flow of *Gevurah*—and one that stems from ego? One way to understand the difference is to look at a craftsperson. A successful artisan often speaks of having real respect for the materials. This is in marked contrast with the perception that to master an art we must have "power" over the materials we use. The distinction lies in our focus. Are we focused on conquest or upon achieving a unity with the Cosmos through our deeds?

For *Gevurah* to possess the attribute of selflessness, it has to be other-centered. A pure spiritual endeavor has the same quality. Spiritual seekers can spend years seeking enlightenment and yet remain untouched. They remain preoccupied with self, and the spiritual work becomes a tool with which to inflate themselves. We have all met people who are proficient in a discipline, who have gained mastery of some of the tools of enlightenment, but who have not gained mastery of themselves. We see here the *Nefesh Behamit,* the lower-order self at play, in which, sadly, the *Gevurah* discipline becomes an end in itself.

How can we tell if our *Gevurah* is coming from the higher dimension of *Nefesh Elokit*? The clue lies in our focus. We must ask ourselves, "Is my focus on how good I am? Am I concerned with how I appear to the world? If these are the primary goals, then the *Gevurah* is tainted. If we seek to acquire self-awareness and effect a transformation that is not ego based, but stems from the joy and happiness of giving and contributing—then the *Gevurah* filters through the higher-order self—the *Nefesh Elokit*—and is pure. There is nothing intrinsically egotistical about being happy, joyful, and fulfilled—if it is the by-product and not the aim.

The Value and Pain of Holding Back

We have all learned the wisdom of selectively holding back. Our *Gevurah* flow is healthy when it protects us from falling backward into the deep end of the pool, when it protects us from putting our hand in the fire or stepping into oncoming traffic on a busy street. Likewise we hold back feelings when trust is lacking, when we have felt the pain of being taken advantage of or mocked. We pull away from shady business transactions and questionable business practices because we know that somewhere along the line emotional or spiritual pain will result.

But sometimes the pain is too much, and then we mistrust and fear the world. We allow our *Gevurah* to flow too quickly, too strongly, too habitually. We constantly need to feel safe and to seek to control others. We may try to dominate and cajole. We approach life anticipating pain in every encounter.

This misguided flow of *Gevurah* can imprison us and cut us off from the possibility of self-fulfillment.

Kabbalah teaches us that fear is the opposite of love.

And just as love is the product of *Hessed,* so is fear the product of *Gevurah.* Both love and fear can be expressed wisely or unwisely. Unbalanced love can suffocate. Unhealthy fear produces worry and uncertainty. It creates a need for control and a perceived vulnerability. It can inflict pain and hurt.

Do not confuse fear with hate. Hate can be a perverted form of connection. To hate means to be connected to someone else in the worst possible way. Fear, however, always disconnects. When we are afraid we run away or we seek safety by control and domination. People who are customarily fearful can become controlling to ensure that they have access to an escape route at all times.

We can see that the flow of *Gevurah* can be tricky. We need to become comfortable with it, both intellectually and experientially, in order to achieve inner balance and maintain healthy relationships.

The Work of *Avoido*—Spiritual Mastery

A younger evolving Hassid is taught that all the theory in the world is of no use without *avoido.* Literally, this means "work." It consists of the work of changing oneself. The Hassidic master is the embodiment of the realized person. *Avoido* is the means by which the student trains the Mind and Emotion flows and behaviors to embody the attributes that the master demonstrates in his life.

The basis of *avoido* is self-containment and self-effacement. This requires a strong flow of *Gevurah*—holding back. Born with a full complement of inclinations, urges, natures, and wants, we as children naturally seek means of expression that are usually basic self-gratification. That is why a child wants and wants and wants. We call this childish tendency *mochin dekatnus*—being "small-brained." The soul is complete from the moment of birth, but the body—and specifically the brain—has not fully developed. Hence the soul is imperfectly expressed through the brain. The spiritual aptitudes of Mind and Emotion cannot operate optimally. As we mature we learn to stop wanting indiscriminately. We learn to control our appetites and to transform our primitive needs into a giving posture.

In the Kabbalistic tradition we are taught that the body completes its organic growth at bar mitzvah for a boy (thirteenth birthday) and bat mitzvah for a girl (twelfth birthday). This is when maturity and inner balance finally establishes itself. At this stage a Jewish boy and girl assume full responsibility for their actions and behaviors. At this stage *avoido* can begin to be practiced, as the physiology has caught up with the soul's fullness. This is the age when delayed gratification and the other behaviors signaling maturity can begin to function. But, these can't function if we don't allow them to—if we don't "wisen up" or "grow up." And the basic tool for maturity through *Gevurah* is holding back, creating space for wisdom to arise, withholding selfish wants and desires, and taming these toward higher ends. The basic work, *avoido,* is that of mastering the flow of *Gevurah.*

The *rebbe,* the Hassidic master, who can see into the dynamic of soul in body, can advise a seeker what *avoido* practices would be optimal for the total development of self-mastery. He might emphasize mental training through Torah study or emotional training through a practice of giving. Accepting the master's advice, and the resultant discipline training, would entail ego abnegation. This, once again, is achieved through the masterful flow of *Gevurah.*

Isaac—A Paradigm of *Gevurah*

If Abraham is the paradigm of *Hessed,* his son Isaac is certainly the paradigm of *Gevurah.* The Bible tells us that like his father, Isaac was a desert dweller; but unlike Abraham, he did not rebel against the mores of society, wage wars, or carve out new territories. The Torah describes him as a "well-digger." This description belies his actual contribution. Isaac was the great consolidator. He redug the wells that his father had uncovered and which the Philistines had, in the interim, filled up. He worked in the shadow of his charismatic father, quietly consolidating what Abraham had initiated. We can only imagine his level of self-containment, dedication, and discipline—hallmarks of the *Sefira* of *Gevurah*. A story is told that illustrates his powerful balance between *Hessed* and *Gevurah*. Isaac's daughters-in-law were idol worshipers. He chose to ignore this in order to keep the peace in his household, although it caused him great pain. G-d took pity on Isaac and struck him blind so that he would not witness these heretical practices. Inner strength enabled Isaac to take the long view and to tolerate the intolerable, rather than use his authority as patriarch to drive his daughters-in-law from the house.

GEVURAH VISUALIZATION EXERCISE

Sit in a comfortable chair. Close your eyes and become calm. You are safe.

Enter the room where you experienced and practiced the *Hessed* flow. Walk to the left side of the room, toward the left wall. Allow yourself to feel constricted. You will feel a sense of withdrawal—a holding back. As you approach the wall, the feeling will be more intense. It is not frightening or unpleasant. It is curious.

On the wall you will see another name of the Creator—*Elokim*. In Hebrew the letters add up to eighty-six, the same arithmetical total as the Hebrew word for "nature." This name of G-d screens the higher reality of creation and creates the illusion of a finite material world. This world, as you see it, is its "outer skin." Everything in the world has a skin—an outer layer that hides and protects the living fruit within.

Within you is also a living fruit—the spark of soul. But the soul is surrounded by the "skin" of Mind and Emotion. Touch the left wall and you will feel the soul's inner contraction, pulling in, holding, withdrawing.

In your mind's eye, hold on to the left wall and sense the power of the name of *Elokim*. Recall an occasion when you spoke, instead of keeping a wiser silence. Go back to that moment. Relive it, but allow that inner holding to discipline your tongue. In reliving that moment, see yourself practicing the wisdom of silence, even in the face of provocation. Allow that past moment of history to be rerun but including, this time, the practice of *Gevurah*. Hold back. Create space for wisdom to flow. Allow your *Gevurah* to shape a healing *Hessed* flow. Carefully consider the outcome. Note the virtue of holding back when wisdom dictates silence. Touch the left wall again and feel the power of the *Gevurah* flow. Recall another occasion when you might have held back and not having done so caused hurt. Again, replay the occasion, this time allowing your wisdom to guide your *Gevurah* flow. Allow yourself to see the new outcome.

Slowly move away from the left wall. You can already sense the power of the *Gevurah* flow waning. It doesn't feel like emptiness. It just provides space for other emotions to enter. Move your fingers and toes and come back into the "real" world.

ם מ

A MEDITATION ON THE LETTER
MEM SOFEET

ם

MEM
SOFEET

Mem sofeet *represents perfection and completion. Its form is sealed, and like* Gevurah, *it is withholding. Meditate on positive aspects of withholding, that of inner strength and self-containment. The* mem sofeet *makes a humming "m" sound. It holds the breath within. Meditate on the quiet sound.*

When *Hessed* and *Gevurah* are balanced the result is spiritual beauty that glows as inner fulfillment and harmony—a harmony described in the next *Sefira,* the *Sefira* of *Tif'eret*—the beauty of balance.

10

Tif'eret: Growing a Wise Heart

The great twelfth-century physician and philosopher Moses Maimonides counseled his disciples to always seek the middle path. Interestingly, he advised people who were angry or stingy to go to extremes. He told an angry person to become a peacemaker, even when it seemed to contradict logic, and he advised a miserly man to struggle with his instincts and give more than he could afford. As we have seen in the past two chapters, anger and stinginess are the very antitheses of the giving nature of the Cosmos.

The following Hassidic tale illustrates this precept: Once upon a time a king had two close friends who rebelled against the kingdom. The king seemed to have no choice but to execute the law—the death penalty. But he could not bring himself to kill his friends. Instead he erected a tightrope over the courtyard at a precarious height. Each prisoner was allowed to walk across the tightrope to freedom. The chances were slim, yet miraculously the first prisoner succeeded. The second prisoner called out to his friend for advice, and the freed man obliged. He called back, "Whenever I felt myself beginning to list to one side I didn't wait until my weight was there but immediately compensated."

This is Maimonides's advice. Don't wait until your words and behavior reveal an imbalance of emotion. Compensate even before the expressions become visible. This is the pathway to emotional balance achieved through the *Sefirah* of *Tif'eret.*

Inner Balance for Wellness

All spiritual pathways advocate inner balance. It is also the underlying posture in the Eastern Ayurvedic medical approach that Deepak Chopra made accessible.

The Ayurvedic approach to wellness sees our basic nature in terms of three basic body types, called *doshas,* that combine in ten possible ways. The combinations result in ten subsets of typologies by which, individually, we can be assessed. These typologies are inherited, resulting in a "signature package" of mind, body, and behavior. Generalizations can be made about each typology. For example, the *vata* types tend to be thin, quick, light sleepers, excitable, worriers, and prone to quick energy bursts. *Pitta* types tend to be of medium build, possessing sharp wit and intellect, more easily angered, articulate, and orderly with meals. *Kapha* types tend to be strongly built, relaxed, grasp information more slowly, are more tolerant, and sleep longer hours.

Much of Ayurvedic treatment centers around restoring each *dosha* to his or her self. The emphasis is on reinstating a healthy balance in the individual in whom the natural equilibrium has been disturbed by a dislocation in lifestyle and Mind-Emotion. A very good book that introduces these concepts and the Ayurvedic model is *Perfect Health: The Complete Mind/Body Guide* by Deepak Chopra.

The interesting parallel with Kabbalah and Hassidic psychology is the idea that we have the power to consciously intervene and alter the unbalanced state. Both systems teach that the Mind has a powerful influence on our spiritual and physical balances.

The Ayurvedic tradition calls the original natural balance of a person *prakriti*—the one found at birth. The

Kabbalistic tradition talks of complex criteria for original balance going back to the moment of conception. In both traditions it is understood that the self-talk of life can alter this natural balance, requiring remedial practices and approaches. Hassidism teaches that everything about our inner dynamics and outer behavior can be changed through conscious intervention of Mind—through a reinterpretation of the moments of life.

A creative individual, a *chochom*, may express the gift impulsively and may need balancing of the *Chochma* flow of creativity with the remedial practice of contemplation (*Bina*). A cogent thinker, a *mayvin*, may become cold and calculating and need rebalancing of the *Bina* flow through greater emotional expression that can be elicited through the practice of *Da'at*. A practical individual, a *da'atan*, is in danger of becoming a heartless technocrat and would require a rebalancing of the *Da'at* flow through the activity of giving—the *Hessed* flow. Maimonides teaches us that a balance sometimes requires a deliberate behavior toward its opposite.

Moses Maimonides was a brilliant medieval physician. Among his remedies were the use of hydrotherapy, specific food combination, exercise, pleasant surroundings, meditation, seasonal fruits, and even the direction that the beds face (a touch of feng shui?).

The Flow of Compassion

If we could not achieve harmony between our giving and withholding natures, our inner emotional climate would be chaotic. We would constantly be in a state of war with ourselves. Without balance we would find our *Hessed* flow overpowering our *Gevurah,* or vice versa. Of course, we all have experienced some level of emotional indecision and the physical exhaustion that accompanies it. By and large most of us are able to resolve the dilemma through the flow of *Tif'eret.* In individuals whose flow of *Tif'eret* is lacking or untrained, this issue becomes a real emotional problem that requires guidance and counseling.

The *Sefira* of *Tif'eret* provides a harmonizing influence. It blends *Hessed* and *Gevurah* just as *Da'at* balances *Chochma* and *Bina. Da'at* results in the harmony and creativity of thought development. *Tif'eret* results in compassion. Compassion is not a simple feeling, but a composite of many elements. Compassion arises when we choose to give, despite circumstances that might not warrant it. For example, a judge may weigh circumstances and choose compassion over harsh judgment. Parents who understand that their child's disruptive behavior is a result of emotional upheaval may choose to be compassionate rather than punitive. A benefactor may be compassionate in his contribution to a man who has poor financial management skills yet struggles to overcome his limitations.

In each of these instances we see an element of withdrawal. The judge understands that a crime has been committed, the parent understands that the child has been rude, and the benefactor understands that mismanagement of funds has occurred. But at the same time, this *Gevurah* withdrawal from the unacceptable behavior finds compensation through the *Hessed* bond of connection and empathy. *Tif'eret* fuses the two flows. Ideally it favors *Hessed* and kindness, resulting in a new amalgamation. Just as a painter combines the primary colors of blue and yellow to form a new color, green, so too compassion is the result of the need for discipline and management softened and modulated by kindness and open-heartedness. If we were to withdraw *Gevurah* from the mix, we would be left with giving that was undirected and undisciplined, giving without sense or balance. On the other hand, if we were to delete *Hessed*, we would be left with a bitter brew of harsh discipline and rigid withholding.

Compassion is not weakness. It is strength.
Tif'eret provides the opportunity to create an
emotional balance in the moment.

151

A *TIF'ERET* EXERCISE

Reenter the room. Walk to the right wall and feel the giving flow—*Hessed.* Allow yourself some time to experience that free flow again. Now walk over to the left wall and sense the feeling of withdrawal into your emotional cocoon. Give yourself the opportunity to become familiar with a feeling that is turned inward rather than outward.

Now move toward the center of the room. In the center you are aware of the two flows, from your right and from your left. Experience the *Hessed* flow on your right through an angelic force gently prodding you—the angel Michael. Observe your giving flow being coaxed by Michael. Feel Michael's power as soft as water and associate it with the color pale blue.

Now experience the *Gevurah* flow on your left through an angelic force gently tugging at you—the angel Gavriel. Feel Gavriel's force as a fire and associate it with the color yellow orange. You recoil within.

Now allow the fire and water to mingle within. The fires of *Gevurah* are being quenched, and the water of *Hessed* is being warmed. Now you can sensate in a general warmth that spreads throughout your body. Feel it extending from your center, your heart, and radiating throughout your torso, your limbs, right through to your extremities. The warmth feels trusting and homey. Spend a few moments enjoying the warmth of *Tif'eret*.

Bring to mind somebody whom you admonished recently. It might have been a family member or someone in the workplace, or possibly a friend. As you do, you will momentarily sense the fires of *Gevurah*. But immediately move back into your center—the pleasant warmth of *Tif'eret*. Find a plausible reason for the person's misbehavior or mismanagement. Allow that reason to settle in your heart. While you focus on that person in your mind, see yourself projecting your warmth as waves of compassion. Allow the warmth of compassion to subdue the egocentric hurt that you felt. See the person experiencing your compassionate warmth. Allow a smile to arise on that person's face. Allow yourself an inner smile as well.

Repeat the exercise with another incident, another person—another occasion.

Now look inside your spiritual heart. See the beauty of color—a soft green of newly sown grass. The innocent beauty of the tender blades can almost be felt with your total being. Allow yourself to be nourished by the softness of touch and color. Prepare to leave the room. Begin moving your fingers and toes where you are seated. Come back into the here and now.

Discovering the Softness of Heart

The term *rachamim* literally means "compassion." *Rachamim* is related to the Hebrew word for "womb," *rechem.* Despite the pain of childbirth, a mother establishes an invincible bond with her child that overcomes the disenchantment and anger that child rearing often brings. (Of course, today sex-typed responses are becoming less significant, as men learn to honor their feminine side.)

As we know, compassion is a most beautiful feeling, and *Tif'eret* literally means "beauty." In her book *Kitchen Table Wisdom,* Rachel Naomi Remen recalls the healing work she did with a Holocaust survivor, whose response to the enormity of the spiritual pain he lived with was to close off feelings toward people and to be "cautious with his heart." Dr. Remen relates that he joined her on retreat after he was diagnosed with cancer. Initially he was belligerent to strangers, but through inner stillness exercises and introspection he had a transformational experience. One day, while meditating, he sensed a deep pinkish light emanating from his chest. He felt enclosed by a beautiful rose. Troubled by the experience, he took a walk on the beach and began a silent dialogue with G-d. He asked the Creator whether it is all right to love strangers. G-d's answer jolted him: "You

A STAR OF DAVID MEDITATION

Breathe in. Become aware of your senses. Recognize your taste buds by rubbing your tongue along your upper and lower teeth. Allow the scent of the room to penetrate your being. What sounds are entering your consciousness? What are your fingers touching? Where are your eyes focusing? Close them. Allow thoughts to pass through you gently with no prompting or urgency. You are safe.

With your eyes closed, envision a beautiful lawn shaped like a huge six-sided Star of David. You are walking on the grass. You are lifted up by a breeze. Find yourself resting lightly on a huge rose petal. Feel its softness and gentleness. The breeze lifts the petal lightly, and you feel the sensation of its inner life—its symbiotic relationship with nature. Sense its power to grow, to bloom, and to close. Note your own power to develop, grow, and spiritually mature. Identify with the flower. You are the flower.

make strangers, I don't." In that instant, the Holocaust survivor's feeling of interpersonal distance began to melt. Strangers were no longer strangers. It was all right to love a stranger.

The Kabbalah tells us that *Hessed* flow is white and that *Gevurah* is red. The two produce pink. Perhaps it was the pink light of *Tif'eret* that shone from his heart. Extending the imagery, we note that the rose has thirteen petals. In Kabbalah, G-d's compassion is expressed through a thirteen-worded sequence, which forms part of the Jewish prayer said on the holy days. The thirteen petals enclosed the ailing Holocaust survivor in a pink cocoon.

Dancing a Pas de Deux of Emotion

What is your perception of beauty? Does a Matisse painting, with its vivid blend of deep colors and short brush strokes, rivet you? Or is it a brilliant desert sunset that moves you? Maybe you know someone larger than life whose faith in the face of adversity and dedication to the welfare of others inspires you. Or perhaps it is the elegance of a simple scientific formula. Our emotions seek balance.

We aspire to goodness, to poise and grace, an inner as well as an outer beauty—a flowing *Sefira* of *Tif'eret*. Hassidic masters teach us that whatever our eyes see is a deliberate teaching tool of the Cosmos. Here is a teaching:

> Sunset is the final moment when the sun bows down and pays homage to its Creator. The day's passage of the sun across the sky is its genuflection. The last moments of its expression of humility are symbolic of the whole of nature. The insects begin to sing their praises of joy. The birds streak briskly from tree to tree, chirping in unison. An air of expectancy permeates the moment. The breeze stills. Meanwhile, the blueness of a summer sky becomes filtered with pinks, which magically transform into crimsons. As the fiery sun sinks into the ocean, the purples and blacks begin to herald the royal exit. Just as the sun's ego ceases to be, it is granted a rebirth. Trillions of its star-children, sparkling through the deep blue velvet cover, envelop our orb of vision. The day and night flow into each other in the same way that *Hessed* and *Gevurah* coalesce into the beauty of *Tif'eret*—all in the soul of humankind.

When we meditate on the way that nature pays homage to the Creator, we create the same beauty within. The pas de deux of *Hessed* and *Gevurah,* dancing in perfect harmony, become the new balance of *Tif'eret.*

The wise choice of actions and words also express the beauty of the *Tif'eret* flow. Our loving inclination to give must be balanced by the strength of restraint to match the capacity of the receiver. Words that are too effusive and too strong may create discomfort instead of closeness. Enthusiasm must be matched by caution, or we may frighten the birds we are trying to feed. When the ideal balance is achieved, we have an expression of beauty through the medium of *Tif'eret*. Inner balance is reflected in outer physical beauty. The nose may be too long, the eyes a little small, and the ears too large, yet the total effect can be one of remarkable beauty. Beauty lies not in the individual component parts, but in their sum total. And the perception of the viewer is part of that truth. Connecting (*Hessed*) and objectifying (*Gevurah*) result in a new perception. That is the beauty of *Tif'eret*.

Beauty and Truth

Hassidism also explains *Tif'eret* as the quality of truth. Truth, we are taught, is the picture that emerges when all the composite pieces are put together. We look at a person and sometimes see perplexing and disconcerting dissonance. The person is good, kind, and caring in professional life and mean, short-tempered, and unfeeling in private. Why should this be? It is when we discover that person's truth, the reason for the dissonance, that the healing can begin.

I recall someone telling me that all behavior is reasonable, without exception, in the sense that a reason lurks behind all of them. All combinations of behavior and expression reveal an inner truth. In fact, the Hebrew word for "truth" is *emet.* The first letter of the word is *aleph,* which is also the first letter of the Hebrew alphabet. The final letter is *tav*—the final letter of the alphabet. The middle letter, *mem,* is at the very center. We learn from Hassidic teachings that while not all things are separately true, truth does lie in the integration of all the composite parts from beginning to end, including the elements in between.

Nature possesses many truths. Scholars engage in scientific endeavor, philosophical speculation, historical study—all seeking eternal truths. The Creator hides these truths just out of reach of human comprehension, eliciting from us the eternal quest—the Cosmic game of hide-and-seek. When we play hide-and-seek we enjoy the game only because somebody is looking for us. There is no point in hiding if no one is seeking. The cleverer our hiding place, the greater the challenge. The Cosmos plays the same game. The harder we search for life's beauty, the greater the joy of discovery. The more profound the truth, the greater the Creator's joy at being found. The moment of discovery is the sweetest and most beautiful of all. A unity is achieved and another face of truth revealed.

Hessed seeks. *Gevurah* hides. *Tif'eret* finds.

The Paradigm of *Tif'eret*

The patriarch Jacob is associated with the paradigm of *Tif'eret*. Remember that it was Jacob who fooled his blind father, Isaac, into giving him the birthright blessing that belonged to his older brother, Esau. The Bible tells us that he came before his father dressed in a special garment that had been passed down through the ages from the original hunter, Cain. Whoever wore it had dominion over the animal kingdom. The garment was incredibly beautiful and covered with lifelike pictures of G-d's wild creatures.

We see that Jacob, a man of learning and contempla-

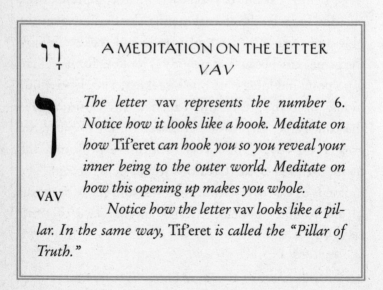

וָו

A MEDITATION ON THE LETTER
VAV

VAV

The letter vav *represents the number 6. Notice how it looks like a hook. Meditate on how* Tif'eret *can hook you so you reveal your inner being to the outer world. Meditate on how this opening up makes you whole.*

   Notice how the letter vav *looks like a pillar. In the same way,* Tif'eret *is called the "Pillar of Truth."*

THE *SEFIROT* AS THREE PILLARS

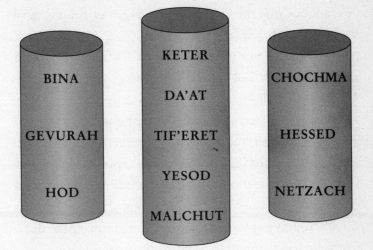

BINA

GEVURAH

HOD

KETER

DA'AT

TIF'ERET

YESOD

MALCHUT

CHOCHMA

HESSED

NETZACH

tion, used a hunter's garment—representing his antithesis, to achieve his goal. Jacob combined the qualities of his practical and peace-loving father, Isaac, with those of his charismatic grandfather Abraham, in that he possessed Abraham's creative spirit and Isaac's dedication. It was Jacob who brought into being the twelve tribes of Israel and became the progenitor of the Jewish people.

In the same way, *Tif'eret* transposes inner Emotions into actual relationships. The *Tanya* observes that Jacob epitomizes the nature of truth—that is, the transposition of potential into actuality. As we saw, *Tif'eret* also represents truth.

Jacob is the focal point of Jewish lineage. Before him came the formative pioneers, his father and grandfather. After him came the twelve tribes. Sages of the mystical tradition call Jacob "the middle bolt."

On the *Sefirotic* table of three pillars, *Tif'eret* remains in the center, in line with *Keter, Yesod,* and *Malchut*— "the middle bolt."

So far, we have discussed emotional dispositions. *Hessed, Gevurah,* and *Tif'eret* do not reach out. They are internal Emotions. They can become expressed in the real world only via relationships with the aide of the next triad of *Sefirotic* flows: *Netzach, Hod,* and *Yesod.* The next three chapters explore the nature of relationships and the overt manifestation of the Mind/Heart combination.

Let us begin with *Netzach* and explore the quest to enter into a relationship with another.

11

❧

Netzach: Initiating Meaningful Relationships

Actualizing Feelings

A young man once approached Albert Einstein and asked the scientist to explain the theory of relativity. Einstein inquired if the man knew any math. The answer was no. He then asked the young man if he knew any physics. Again, the answer was no. Undaunted, Einstein reduced the theory to the following sentence: "If you are sitting on a sofa with your girlfriend for a full hour, it will seem like minutes, but if you sit on a hot stove for minutes, it will feel like a full hour."

In order for us to communicate effectively, the information has to be transmitted in an accessible manner. We must negotiate across differences of backgrounds, cultures, and values. How can I make someone understand and feel my perspective? Why do some people leave a greater impact than others? How do we protect the compassion of *Tif'eret* from being misunderstood? The answers to these questions lie in the *Sefirotic* flow of *Netzach*.

Netzach represents our sincere desire to overcome the barriers that exist between individuals. It represents our desire to engage in meaningful relationships.

The Tools of Relationship

We are now familiar with six spiritual tools. *Chochma* draws on our creativity and our inspiration. *Bina* allows them to be configured into cogent thought patterns. *Da'at* combines the two but allows them to give birth to Emotion. These three, *Chochma, Bina,* and *Da'at,* are the tools of the Mind.

We have also seen the tools of Emotion. *Hessed* promotes the powerful feeling of giving and sharing. *Gevurah* restrains this flow. *Tif'eret* blends them into a cogent and total feeling that can now be expressed without the tension of inner duality.

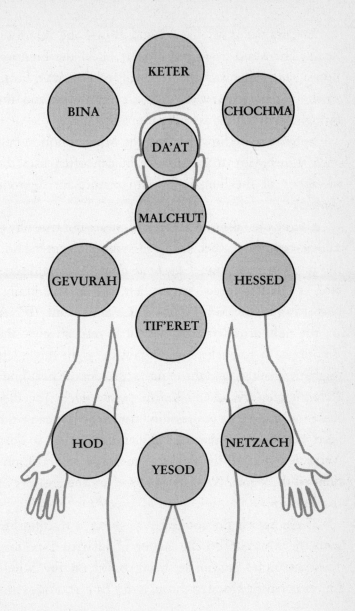

In summary, we have Mind flows and Emotion flows. The Mind flows can directly affect the Emotion flows. Think one way and you will feel that way. It can work in reverse as well—feel a certain way and the thoughts will follow, as with rationalization.

Four *Sefirotic* flows express the Mind-Emotion balance as behavior and action. Kabbalah often uses the metaphor of the human form to picture the *Sefirotic* centers.

Unlike the Eastern *Chakras,* these are not true physiologic centers. Rather, they are symbolic centers, and the body is metaphor. *Chochma-Bina-Da'at* (abbreviated as *Chabad*) are the right, left, and middle brains, respectively—the Mind. *Hessed, Gevurah,* and *Tif'eret* are the right arm, left arm, and torso, respectively—the Emotions. In Kabbalistic metaphor, the right thigh, left thigh, the genitals, and the mouth represent the next four: *Netzach, Hod, Yesod,* and *Malchut,* respectively. Together these four represent Expression. Just as the feet carry the head and feelings to the place of their destination, so does *Netzach* and *Hod,* the thighs, take the Mind and Emotions to their goal. *Netzach* and *Hod* are the creators of relationship.

These *Sefirot* do not enjoy as direct a relationship with the Mind as do the *Sefirot* of internal Emotion. They are more automatic, being based on the Mind-Emotion balance located through the *Tif'eret.* For example, the feet automatically take the head where the head wants to go. Being automatic, these *Sefirot* are somewhat more difficult to master. For example, nonverbal behav-

---

A STAR OF DAVID MEDITATION

Breathe in. Become aware of your senses. Recognize your taste buds by rubbing your tongue along your upper and lower teeth. Allow the scent of the room to penetrate your being. What sounds are entering your consciousness? What are your fingers touching? Where are your eyes focusing? Close them. Allow thoughts to pass through you gently with no prompting or urgency. You are safe. With your eyes closed, envision a beautiful lawn shaped like a huge six-sided Star of David. You are walking on the grass. From a distance you spy a lion. Notice its majesty and regal bearing. It glides along, oblivious of you. Recognize its courage. Identify with the lion. Become aware of your own majesty, your own regal bearing in the domain of the kingdom of your Mind and Heart. You too can be the king of your spiritual jungle. Contemplate on this for a moment.

---

ior is more difficult to control and change than conscious thoughts or feelings, and as you may have experienced, body habits are notoriously difficult to alter.

Another interesting point is that *Netzach, Hod,* and *Yesod* also correlate with *Hessed, Gevurah,* and *Tif'eret.* Just as *Hessed* is the *Sefira* of giving, so *Netzach* is the *Sefira* of reaching out. Just as *Gevurah* is the flow of restraint and discipline, so *Hod* is the flow of limiting the process of reaching out. In the same way that *Tif'eret* creates a balance of *Hessed* and *Gevurah, Yesod* creates a balance of *Netzach* and *Hod.* While it would be incorrect to see *Netzach* as a direct conduit for, or an extension of, *Hessed,* they do enjoy some similarities, and in the column of the *Sefirot, Netzach* lies below *Hessed* and *Hod* lies below *Gevurah.*

Netzach, translated from Hebrew, means "Victory" or "Enduring"—the idea of being victorious in crossing the interpersonal boundaries—reaching out and entering into a relationship. It is "enduring" in the sense that it successfully overcomes our natural resistance to opening ourselves up to another.

Reaching Out Requires Spiritual Thrust

When we wake up on a cold morning, it takes willpower to relinquish the blankets and put our feet on the floor.

Once we've pulled ourselves out, the rest is much easier.

Likewise, reaching out and making a connection requires effort and courage. We feel safe in our emotional cocoon, and the decision to open up and share requires courage. It can be troublesome, tiresome, frightening, and sometimes painful. But, like leaving the comfort of a safe, warm bed, once we have made the effort, worlds open up to us.

Many relationships fail because we are simply unaware of our inner dynamics. For example, the pace and the growth of a relationship depends on how openly we behave toward one another. We must learn how to initiate the flow of feelings. We must learn how to negotiate the boundary of our differences. This calls upon insights into the nature of the *Sefira* of *Netzach.*

> The main thing is not to be afraid.
> —REB NACHMAN OF BRATZLAV

The Angst of Fear

Hassidic master Reb Nachman of Bratzlav compared life to a narrow bridge. To cross it successfully we must put aside our fears. We must have our eyes fixed firmly on the other side, and *we must keep moving. Netzach* is our capacity to overcome the barriers that exist between us.

Netzach is our ability to accept the challenge. *Netzach* allows the feelings to keep moving. *Netzach* allows for a duet, a partnership, a friendship, and love's expression.

Sometimes we are afraid to make the transition from internal feelings to outward expression. Perhaps we have experienced rejection in response to our disclosure of intimate feelings. Pain has caused us to withhold our feelings and imprison our *Netzach* potential. Everyone has seen naturally exuberant children become reclusive teenagers and noncommunicative adults.

Fear depresses the flow of Netzach.

Relationships cannot flourish in its absence.

I and Thou

Martin Buber was an assimilated Jew who became enraptured by stories of the Hassidic masters and their spiritual followers. The philosophy of Hassidism became his lifelong pursuit, and after immigrating from prewar Europe to Israel, he became a professor at the Hebrew University in Jerusalem.

Buber based his philosophy on the Hassidic masters, and his books have attracted a worldwide audience of both Jews and non-Jews. In one of his major works, titled *I and Thou,* he discusses two types of relationships. He calls one type the I-It relationship, and it represents a relationship in which one person regards the other as the means to fulfill an end. The relationship may be friendly, but it is also "user" oriented.

Buber calls the second type of relationship I-Thou. This relationship is one of mutual respect and acceptance. We encounter the other as an infinitely valuable whole. The I-Thou relationship is about making the secular sacred and sanctifying our relationships.

> The way to relate optimally to a person is "as
> an end also, and never as a means."
> —EMMANUEL KANT

The I-Thou insight informs us that to cross the interpersonal boundary we have to accept where the other person is and how that person is. We must accord the individual respect through humility.

Buber captured the essence of the *Netzach* flow through his I-Thou philosophy. *Netzach* seeks to touch the being of the other, through a relationship of profound respect and mutual engagement. It is a relationship of sharing rather than achieving at another person's expense.

Kabbalah might translate the idea of I-Thou as the recognition that every person possesses a divine spark— a soul. For when we recognize the essential holiness and infinite value that we all possess, we are naturally moved to profound respect. To use another for our own ends becomes not only disdainful and disrespectful, but also sacrilegious.

So while *Netzach* represents engagement in the space of another, it must be channeled through the higher-order self, the *Nefesh Elokit*, in order to be of the I-Thou variety rather than the lower, manipulative expression of I-It.

Beyond the Ego Boundary

Psychology tells us a great deal about the nature of relationships. We are told that when we are born we cannot distinguish between self and other. The room, our mother's face, the bedsheet—all are perceived as extensions of ourselves. But by the age of one we discover primitive boundaries. We are a separate entity. Knowing where we begin and end is called "the ego boundary." But some aspects are still blurred. Even at two years of age we are still not aware of limitations. We make constant demands and seek to control everything—the "terrible twos." From the age of three onward we develop an understanding of our powerlessness in the real world, although we continue to fantasize about being all-powerful through our games.

In *The Road Less Traveled,* M. Scott Peck points out that we are lonely behind our ego boundaries. We yearn to escape and explore the world of another. We want to leave our personal limits. Herein lies the quest for relationships. All relationships express the *Netzach* urge to seek out a world beyond our boundaries. Even in our early experiences, our sense of anxiousness or comfort varies. If initial attempts have proven to be painful, the *Netzach* flow can be stunted and we engage in fantasy.

When *Hessed* flows strongly through the funnel of a balanced *Tif'eret, Netzach* will actualize the flow by extending the ego boundary to envelop the other. In other words, you feel for the other person as much as you feel for yourself. This is called true love.

This love, the I-Thou relationship, can be expressed in many ways. For example, we can love a garden with a care and devotion that is palpable and real. We can treat the seedlings with tenderness that is usually accorded newborn infants and feed the soil with the same gentleness a parent exhibits when feeding a young child. We might feel as protective of the sapling as we would of a son or daughter. The *Netzach* flows freely as we weed, trim, and prune. That love will unite the gardener and garden. The boundary encloses both.

When the purpose of gardening is merely to create a showpiece to impress others, there is less tenderness and connection. Under those circumstances the ego boundary has not stretched to encompass the garden, and it represents Buber's I-It relationship—using the garden as a tool for ulterior motives. In this case the *Netzach* flows, but *it is a flow that is directed to the ones who are to be impressed—not to the garden itself.* It is also flowing through the lower-order self, the *Nefesh Behamit,* seeking to shore up some inadequacy or a perceived shortcoming that results in the need to impress others.

The *Netzach* flow is the spiritual key to our successful exploration beyond the ego boundary, but like any tool, it can be used to benefit or harm. A teacher can inadvertently dominate the classroom because of an overabundance of enthusiasm. A partner may be so effusive that the relationship is spoiled by an inability to listen. *Netzach* is a two-edged sword. It provides the drive to actuate a feeling. In a less balanced individual, however, it can also lead to domination and the quest for control and power.

Why is power and control so attractive to many? Lacking self-esteem and self-worth, some people try to fill their "black hole" of inadequacy through artificial self-aggrandizement. They are afraid of their perceived shortcomings and feel a deep lack of wholeness. The *Tif'eret* potential (a feeling of balanced contribution) is not harnessed, and the *Netzach* flow becomes perverse in its rush to compensate. In its desire to connect and unify, *Netzach* flows too strongly, callously, unmindful of the other, straining to fill the void within. The behavior becomes overpowering and dominating.

The Paradigm of *Netzach*

Kabbalah teaches that Moses epitomizes the *Sefira* of *Netzach*. Moses was the intermediary in the Hebrews' relationship with G-d. In fact, relationship was at the core of his spiritual leadership and his personal being. When he was a prince in Egypt, Moses came to the defense of a Hebrew being attacked by his Egyptian taskmaster. Later he overcame the power of Pharaoh and aggressively led the population of over four million Hebrews for forty years. When we observe his life's trajectory, we can see that Moses was the energy of *Netzach* personified.

NETZACH EXERCISES

EXERCISE 1:
Go outside to a place you can walk around freely. Find an inanimate object at least twenty yards away that attracts your interest. Begin walking very slowly toward it—four to five seconds per step. As you walk, become aware of your thoughts and your feelings as they relate to the movement of your thighs, legs, and feet:

- Focus on your thoughts: Where are you going? Why are you going? What is the source of attraction? What does this say to you about you?
- Focus on your feelings: How do you feel about the object? When did this feeling first arise? Can you strengthen the feeling?
- Focus on your feet: What makes your feet move the way they do? Why are your feet taking you toward that particular object? Can you change your walking style to reflect the character of this particular object?
- As you walk slowly, become aware how a part of you is reaching out to the object. This part of you is somehow intricately interwoven with your Mind and Emotions. Yet your feet move without obvious consciousness of this reaching-out process.
- Allow that consciousness to seep into your style of moving. Exaggerate it somewhat just so that your conscious awareness becomes discernible in the way you walk.
- In this way you begin to master your *Netzach* flow.

Repeat the exercise with another object in mind and with another part of your body—your hands. Identify something that you would like to touch, feel, or hold. Very slowly, no faster than half an inch per second, begin reaching out to touch or hold that object. As you do so, go through the three sets of questions you had with your foot movements, but apply them to the movement of the hands. When you have reached your object allow yourself a few moments to recognize something about your *Netzach* flow—the way you reached out. Do the exercise two or three times a day for about fifteen minutes each day for a week. You will make some very important discoveries about your *Netzach* flow: you will discover how you reach goals, reach out to people, and generally interrelate with life.

Further variations on the theme include how you see with your eyes, taste with your tongue, or hear with your ears. Feel free to create similar exercises for these.

After a few sessions you will find that you are becoming very familiar with your *Netzach* flow, to the extent that you can actually change the mechanism of its flow to something that you are more comfortable with or desire more.

EXERCISE 2.

Sit in a comfortable chair and relax. You are safe. Close your eyes and visualize a room that enfolds many emotions. As you enter, feel these spiritual emotions flowing freely. Move to the right of the room. You will feel a profound desire to reach out, to say or do something with another person or thing. Relax. Recall the exercises you did outside. Feel a strong flow of *Netzach* on the right side of this room, and relive each exercise slowly in your mind. Try to recall every single nuance of the movement of your feet or your hands. Try to relive what you experienced outside, but this time in the right side of the room where your *Netzach* is flowing freely. Allow the subtlest of sensations to be noted. Observe your Mind and Emotions as they interplay in the very moments of the reaching out process. Spend ten minutes in quiet contemplation. Then begin moving your fingers and your toes and return into the here and now.

We must learn to guide the *Netzach* flow or it may be misdirected. The result will be an imbalance in our relationships or, worse still, no relationships. Our willingness to reveal ourselves and share with others must be tempered. We need to know when to speak and when to stay silent. We need to provide ourselves with time and space to assess exactly how we should temper the *Netzach* flow. The next *Sefira*—the *Sefira* of *Hod*, the *Sefira* of empathy and other-centeredness, is the balancing counterpoint of *Netzach*.

זַ יִ ן   ## A MEDITATION ON THE LETTER
ZAYIN

ZAYIN

Zayin represents the number 7. Seven is the number of completion and unity—the seven days of the week, the seven lamps of the menorah, the Sabbatical year. Meditate on the idea of completion. Zayin literally means "weapon."

Just as Netzach *provides the courage to reach out and enter into relationships, the letter* zayin *represents the concept of expanding outward beyond one's comfort zone. Meditate on your courage to reach out beyond yourself. Think of* zayin *and* Netzach *as part of your spiritual armor.*

179

12

Hod:
Creating Empathy

What Shoe Size Do You Wear?

The Mishna tells us not to judge others until we stand in their shoes. And since everyone is born with different spiritual, genetic, and environmental "shoes," it is impossible for us to wear them.

The flow of the *Sefira* of *Hod* is responsible for the creation of space in relationships. It provides the opportunity for the listener to pause and empathize. It allows both listener and initiator to meet on "safe," nonjudgmental territory. Such space facilitates trust and confidence, allowing client, friend, spouse, and child to reveal themselves in a loving manner. To practice *Hod* is to be magnanimous, other-centered, and humble in a relationship. It means resisting the all-too-human temptation to force another's shoes to conform to our feet.

Hod is the counterpoint to *Netzach*. While *Netzach* strives to connect, *Hod* ensures that the power and energy in that striving is appropriate and acceptable. As we said earlier, it makes no sense to impress a student if the information is just too much to assimilate. *Hod* assembles the information to match the capacity of the receiver.

Hod tempers the force of *Netzach,* which, unchecked, can create distance rather than closeness. We have all experienced the colleague who is so effusive about his proposal that people simply stop listening. We have seen good ideas go ignored because an empathetic heart did not balance the *Netzach* exuberance.

> Empathy lies at the core of a caring
> relationship.

A Good Communicator

Hod holds the key to good communication. An effective communicator not only speaks well, but also displays empathic skills. A witty after-dinner speaker may be quite boring in private life. The speaker may perform well while delivering a monologue, but in personal life the gift of true dialogue may be absent. A good public speaker is always aware that he or she is really engaging in dialogue with the audience and throughout the performance shows empathy for the people to whom he or she is speaking.

I learned this lesson during a lecture tour. I had booked a morning plane from New Jersey to Florida, where I was scheduled to give an evening lecture. I gave myself plenty of time, so when fog closed the airport I wasn't concerned. Even when I heard that the incoming flight from Chicago was also shut down, I resigned myself to staying in the airport lounge a little longer. But four o'clock rolled around, and I knew I was in trouble. I finally caught a flight after six P.M. and arrived at the hall an hour and a half late.

The program organizers had been savvy enough to arrange an impromptu activity to keep the audience in their seats. So my audience was there—but they were not happy. I told them how wonderful they were to stay and that if it were me, I would have gone home. They weren't amused. I tried complimenting them and making feeble jokes—all to no avail.

Then I received a flash of divine inspiration. I stopped trying to win them over and began to share myself with them. I told them how uncomfortable I felt. I shared what my thoughts had been during that long day—my anxiety that I might be letting an audience down. And I even managed to get a smile when I pointed out that living in Australia made it somewhat difficult to make amends too quickly. The faces in the audience began to change. I felt them coming over to my side. Finally, the evening turned out to be a great success.

In retrospect, the turning point came when I stopped trying so hard to connect (*Netzach*) and let go of trying to win their approval. Instead I shared myself (*Hod*). The empathy I finally elicited from the audience was the same flow of *Hod* that I was sending out to them.

Hod holds the key to empathic communications. In his book *The Seven Habits of Highly Effective People*, Stephen Covey calls this experience "the skill of empathic listening." He notes the important contradiction of people who want to be understood yet ignore what is happening inside the other person. Most people evaluate, probe, advise, and interpret, but only for their own purposes. The empathy of *Hod* is lacking. A true dialogue is missing.

Covey discusses the Greek philosophy of *Ethos, Pathos,* and *Logos. Logos* represents the logic, *Pathos* the feelings, and *Ethos* the character and relationship. In communication all three play important roles. The three terms raise three unstated but intrinsic questions. Does the speaker make sense (*Logos*)? How does that make the listener feel (*Pathos*)? What is the speaker's credibility rating with me (*Ethos*)? *Ethos* carries the most weight in communication—the credibility factor. If we believe the person, we listen much harder. Then comes feelings (*Pathos*). If we feel for what the speaker says, our involvement in the communication is heightened. Whether it makes sense is surprisingly unimportant (*Logos*).

Our Hassidic model has obvious parallels. The *Sefirotic* flows of Mind are inherent in *Logos*. The flows of inner Emotion are *Pathos*. And the triad of *Sefirotic* flows that facilitate relationships merge to become *Ethos*. So *Netzach, Hod,* and *Yesod,* the *Ethos* factor, are central to effective communication.

Hod becomes the singularly most important *Sefirotic* flow we possess for empathic listening. I won my audience back not because of my wit—the use of *Logos;* nor by playing on their feelings—*Pathos.* We finally communicated because of the empathic flow I initiated by being honest and open about myself—*Ethos.*

The most effective way to display the *Ethos* of *Hod* is to create a safe space into which the other can enter. When we are silent we allow the other to be heard and demonstrate that we care. Naturally the nonverbal behavior must accompany the verbal cues. The eyes must meet and the stance remain open. A good listener does more than shut up and murmur a few platitudes in the appropriate places.

True *Hod* is both nonverbal and behavioral.

Just Saying "Thank You"

How can you learn to create the space of *Hod*?

When I met with the Dalai Lama, he presented me with a number of inscribed books, one of which was entitled *Kindness, Clarity, and Insight: The Fourteenth Dalai Lama,* translated and edited by Jeffrey Hopkins. In that book he talks about the practical preconditions for empathy, something we discussed at length at our meeting. He writes: "In order to have strong consideration for others' happiness and welfare, it is necessary to have a special altruistic attitude in which you take upon yourself the burden of helping others."

This altruism forms the basis of an affirmation that begins each day in the Jewish tradition. It is the basis of a practice that imbues the practitioner with humility and ego abnegation. The Kabbalah explains that this morning affirmation, known as *Modeh Ani,* provides the space to enter into the magical moments characterized by the transition from the unconsciousness of sleep into the light of day. The term *Modeh Ani* is enunciated first thing in the morning. It means "I accept," "I surrender," or "I acknowledge," or "I bow in front of you." It is linked etymologically to the word for "thank you" in Hebrew (*todah*).

This contemplative affirmation acknowledges the wonder and awe of having returned to consciousness, to the here and now. It affirms the opportunity the new day offers to elevate the mundane and to raise Cosmic consciousness and awareness. It surrenders to the responsibility that reawakening thrusts upon us. It invites the Creator into our space. The verb root of both senses, to submit and to say thank you, is also the root of the word *Hod*. The spiritual quality of *Hod* underlines the attributes of humility and acknowledgment.

Properly directed, *Hod* flows through our persona and strips away our facades and projections. *Hod* removes our camouflage of posturing and promotes empathy. It tempers our ego and facilitates the discovery of our true self-worth. It allows us to say "thank you"—an expression of humility.

When we say "thank you" we are withdrawing and creating a comfort zone for another person. We touch their essence and draw it toward us. "Thank you" is a verbalization of the *Hod* flow. That is why it is so important to teach youngsters to say "thank you," even if the deeper import is not yet fully understood. It trains children to express humility and an acknowledgment of others.

People who show humility invite more relationships into their lives. It begins with a simple thank-you.

Self-Esteem and Self-Worth

No two people are identical, just as no two snowflakes have ever fallen with the same geometric structure. Every person is an exquisite thread in the tapestry of life. Each one of us has a function and a purpose that is truly individual and which fully complements the nature of society and of life.

Most of the difficulties people experience come from a blindness to their own individual beauty. Each of us is an indispensable component of creation. Each of us is fully worthy of living at this moment and in this place.

Why do so many people see themselves as unimportant, uninteresting, and unworthy? They believe that pain is the price of not hiding well enough. They do not recognize their true indispensability in the Cosmos.

I honestly believe that if the *Sefira* of *Hod* were consciously adopted in society, if each of us practiced our inner flow of *Hod*, antisocial behavior could be alleviated. *Hod* allows us to step back and recognize the essential, distinctive beauty within ourselves and within others.

I believe that the anger and pain of not being acknowledged or cared for is at the heart of all societal ills. The *Hod* flow of effective listening can produce healthy growth and self-discovery in us all.

Dealing with Adversity

Some people seem to glide smoothly through adversity while others become mired in it and drown. Why? We all experience pain. Yet two people may experience the same pain quite differently. It is as much a product of expectation as it is of objective reality. People who go through life expecting pain will not be disappointed. When we are optimistic, the pain quotient is lessened. When life's pain is filtered through the prism of faith, it is experienced in a more balanced way.

Accepting adversity or pain is an aspect of holding back—a characteristic trait of *Hod*. Instead of feeling angry or cheated and wallowing in our distress, *Hod* allows us to step back and shape the experience into a more positive and meaningful essence.

Submitting to the Flow

Hassidism teaches us that two basic guidelines affect our course in life. The first lies in our gifts—the special qualities that distinguish each of us from the other. The second is the constellation of events around us, over which we have no control. The Ba'al Shem Tov, the founder of Hassidism, teaches us that these are divinely ordained to provide us with the optimal stage upon which to express our life's role. But we fight these events. We seek to control them through our limited wisdom, although we may in fact be doing ourselves a grave disservice.

By fighting our seeming adversities, the Cosmic process of rebalancing invariably results in the rise of even more pressing circumstances that are in truth a corrective mechanism of the Creator. And then war erupts on another front—until we learn the lesson of acceptance. It is more life-enhancing for us to submit our will, not with passive resignation, but in humble acceptance of opportunities as they arise.

Hod molds meaningful acceptance. *Hod* opens us up to the opportunity that adversity provides. It is not to be equated with passivity.

Do we really know what is around the corner? Can we really decide in advance whether an occurrence is going to bring benefit or cause harm? Our only realistic alternative is to remain curious and open, to accept the moment as it arises and follow its development. Adopting a stance of natural curiosity and visualizing a positive outcome raises our tolerance for discomfort. The basis of *Hod* allows the creation of a neutral and accepting stance and the manifestation of a more positive disposition.

To surrender to life's exigencies does not mean that one meekly turns the other cheek. On the contrary, it means that we engage in life fully, that we ride the rhythms of life and sing to the cosmic winds. Choosing our battles carefully enables us to see the forest as well as the trees. We become open to the signposts that direct our own tentative steps.

The secret of the *Sefira* of *Hod* lies in acceptance. It takes a heartfelt thank-you and surrender to the Other to activate submission to the greater wisdom of the Creator. It also takes courage.

A *HOD* EXERCISE

Take out a book with which you are familiar. Open the beginning page of the first chapter and read several paragraphs to yourself. Now repeat by reading aloud, but this time also slow down the reading to the extent that it takes about five seconds to read out the average word. Focus primarily on the sounds the first time you read these few paragraphs. Repeat the exercise, but this time focus on the meaning of the word—only the word you are reading, one word at a time.

Repeat the exercise and focus on the sense of the whole passage as you read out the words.

You may find amazing insights, both in terms of the

content you are reading and within yourself, if you do this exercise once a day for about ten to fifteen minutes. Holding back on the natural inclination to "get ahead" allows the door to depth to open up. Using the capacity of *Hod* this way can assist to change your interpersonal communicative style as well. After doing this exercise for a week, you might want to follow it up with another. Have a partner or friend spend ten minutes a day conversing with you. Choose any topic and simply discuss it. But hold yourself back to a three-second pause before you initiate any conversation or respond to any comment. Only you, not your partner, should practice this restriction. You discover a new level of insight through empathic listening.

Relive the experience of reading from the book. Try to recall the three stages of reading it and the experiences and insights you gained from the exercise. Focus on the value of slowing down response mechanisms and how this deepens your appreciation of things. Once again, try to imprint upon yourself the importance of holding back as a means of deepening your understanding of other people. Bring into focus the opportunity you have created for your *Hod* to flow more freely. Commit yourself to allowing the space of opportunity you have created to continue throughout your life.

My Own Master and the Practice of *Hod*

The Lubavitcher Rebbe was the personification of humility and empathic listening. Throughout his fifty years of spiritual leadership he devoted an astounding twenty hours a day to the service of humanity. He followed no external clock—only the internal cosmic compass that guided him. He frequently held personal audiences throughout the night. My family and I had the honor of being received by the *Rebbe* on one occasion at two o'clock in the morning and on other occasions even closer to dawn. In his later years the *Rebbe* was frail, having survived two heart attacks and other afflictions. Even then he stood for up to six hours every Sunday without moving from the podium that was set up outside his office. Thousands of people approached him one by one, to unburden themselves, to seek a blessing or the solution to a problem.

He responded personally to each individual, and in that moment of profound connection, one felt as if time stood still. I will always remember his eyes meeting mine and the empathy and caring reaching out and touching my mind and heart. The flow of *Hod* was riveting. It felt as though, in the entire universe, only he and I existed. The *Rebbe* absorbed the import of my particular issue and, with extraordinary perceptiveness, responded immediately. I knew that my innermost thoughts had been

A STAR OF DAVID MEDITATION

Breathe in. Become aware of your senses. Recognize your taste buds by rubbing your tongue along your upper and lower teeth. Allow the scent of the room to penetrate your being. What sounds are entering your consciousness? What are your fingers touching? Where are your eyes focusing? Close them. Allow thoughts to pass through you gently with no prompting or urgency. You are safe. With your eyes closed, envision a beautiful lawn shaped like a huge six-sided Star of David. You are walking on the grass.

Think about the archangels as you walk. You sense Michael walking on your right, showering you with compassion. Gavriel walks on your left, providing you with direction and purpose. The archangel Oriel walks in front of you, bringing inner enlightenment. Refael walks behind you, strengthening your own healing capacities. Spend a minute sensing the angelic forces imbuing you with their goodness and gifts.

channeled through the *Rebbe*'s own Mind and Emotions.

It is taught that a *rebbe* can advise because in the process of listening to the petitioner, he assumes their pain and experiences it himself. It is recorded that a number of *rebbes* actually suffered health problems, which they acknowledged was due to this supreme level of empathy. We may not be gifted to the same degree. But we do have the capacity to train our *Hod* to flow in every encounter and in every conversation.

The foremost teacher of Kabbalah and Hassidism,
Rabbi Menachem M. Schneerson o.b.m.—His Eminence,
the Lubavitcher Rebbe. (Itzhak Berez)

The Paradigm of *Hod*

Moses' brother Aaron is the great mediator in Jewish history. The Hebrew word for "peace" is *shalom,* which literally means "the state of completeness through perfect balance." The traditional Hebrew greeting *Shalom Aleichem* in fact means "May you enter into a state of complete inner balance." It is a unique greeting, and it reinforces the major thrust of the spiritual tradition of Kabbalah—self-mastery.

The key to mediation is empathy—what Stephen Covey calls "empathic listening." It is impossible to make peace between people without being able to really listen and hear what each side is saying. Peace means balance, and it is balance that Aaron sought in interpersonal relationships. It is said that Moses was afflicted with a speech impediment that made it difficult for him to speak clearly. His brother not only had the ability to listen with his heart to what people said, but he was also a skillful communicator. For these reasons Aaron is considered the epitome of the *Sefira* of *Hod.*

Mutual acceptance is a basic tenet of any relationship. If the parties do not accept each other, they cannot bond. However, there must also be the *desire* to bond. The Mind and Emotions must penetrate the mask each of us wears. Such bonding is achieved through the next *Sefira,* known as the flow of *Yesod.*

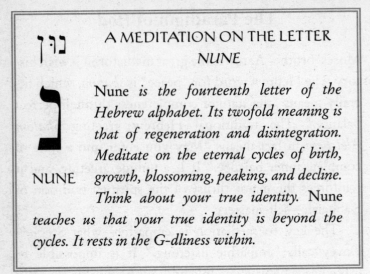

נוּן

נ

NUNE

A MEDITATION ON THE LETTER *NUNE*

Nune is the fourteenth letter of the Hebrew alphabet. Its twofold meaning is that of regeneration and disintegration. Meditate on the eternal cycles of birth, growth, blossoming, peaking, and decline. Think about your true identity. Nune teaches us that your true identity is beyond the cycles. It rests in the G-dliness within.

13

⚬

Yesod:
Achieving a True Bond

The word *Yesod* literally means "foundation." The Kabbalah teaches us that *Yesod* denotes the intensity, bonding, and strength of communication between two people. I remember being excited about a class that was being offered in college. Not only was the subject appealing, but it had the added bonus of being taught by an expert in the field. How disappointed I was to discover that the esteemed expert was an uninspired speaker who buried his face in his notes and droned on for an hour.

Perhaps you remember an occasion in which you

were happily surprised to discover that a lecturer without tenure and speaking extemporaneously inspired an entire audience. In one case, the *Yesod* flow was lacking—notwithstanding the erudition of the professor. In the other, the *Yesod* flowed freely, even though the academic kudos may have been missing. Only the latter speaker left a lasting impression. It is this *Sefira* that creates the foundation upon which human bonding rests.

How many of us can really say that we bond deeply with people? Most of us continue to pursue unfinished agendas and unresolved anger. We flee from insecurity and traumas from past relationships. The focus and dedication we need to pursue deep and meaningful relationships are dissipated. The mind is flooded with myriad concerns, worries, and other competing interests, leaving little space for *Yesod*.

Instead we draw apart, lead separate lives, and lose touch with one another. The key is in strengthening our inner core of wholeness and well-being. Then we can focus on the other—the friend, the partner, the spouse, and our children.

The individuals who most profoundly influence us are the ones who establish a *Yesod* bond with us. When we communicate with such a person we have the sense that we are the most important person in their universe. We feel a closeness, a reciprocity, and the power of true communication.

At the same time, this foundation of *Yesod* is also the harmonizing principle that unites *Netzach* and *Hod*. When the powerful thrust of *Netzach* reaches out from loneliness into a relationship tempered by the restraint of *Hod,* preventing domination and dependency, then the depth of *Yesod* can flow freely. It is the quest for depth and dedication in a relationship that provides the balancing properties of *Netzach* and *Hod*.

However, not all communication is visible or expressed verbally. Words do not always manifest *Yesod*. Nonverbal qualities also create the bond.

What is the nature of this quality? At its core lies the Mind and our ability to focus on the person with whom we are communicating. When we think of focus we naturally think of our sense of sight. However, the focus with which we go about creating meaningful relationships goes beyond the visual. It includes our intent—what Hassidism calls *kavvanah*.

Actually, *kavvanah* represents more than our intent. It includes qualities of dedication, single-mindedness, purpose, goal orientation, and connection. Contiguous with this quality of Mind in *Yesod*, there exists an emotional quality as well. It is our capacity to give and to contribute, empathize and balance. Thus *Yesod* is a funnel for all of the Mind and Emotion *Sefirot* that we have discussed.

We can transmit this focus without words. The

Lubavitcher masters, the *rebbes,* spoke at length about the power of thought. They observed that deeply focused thoughts can literally reach others. When we think well of a person we exercise a therapeutic effect. Unfortunately, when we think ill of a person, we leave our mark as well. In Kabbalistic and Hassidic literature this is known as *ayin hara,* the "evil eye."

Until recently it was fashionable for intellectuals to scoff at the capacity of the human mind to effect change without speech. Larry Dossey, M.D., notes in his book, *Be Careful What You Pray For . . . You Might Just Get It,* a number of interesting experiments that have been carried out, among them one by a research team led by Jacobo Grinberg-Zylberbaum at the Universidad Nacional Autonoma de Mexico. This group examined electroencephalograms (tracings of brain waves) between subjects separated from each other by considerable distance. They discovered that when the subjects allowed a feeling of closeness and awareness to flow between them, the EEG patterns overlapped and distinct correlations were recorded. In defiance of the laws of diminishing effects with greater distance, they found that these patterns did not change as distance was increased. Some scientists call this phenomenon "nonlocal correlation."

Years earlier Einstein first proposed the notion that subatomic particles enter into correlation with one another no matter what distance divides them. Experiments have proven his hypothesis to be true, and it is now being extended to human beings.

Experiments with human beings showed that the EEGs correlated only when there was a deliberate attempt between the parties to be consciously aware of each other—they had to focus on each other. The nonlocal connections took place only when there was focus—when a determined attempt was made to communicate with the other through the mind.

Yesod is also the quality of deeply caring, determined communication. No wonder that the prime example of such *Yesod* flow, that between parent and child, leaves such a powerful effect on the child, even when they are separated geographically.

Nonlocal phenomena have been studied scientifically through observations of *qijong* masters who can make opponents several meters away step backward rapidly without even touching them. The experiments included placing the opponent in a distant, shielded room and observing synchronization of the sender's and receiver's brain waves when the master exercised mental focus.

Dossey also notes the results of experiments from McGill University that showed that mental depression in a gardener can have a negative effect on the growth of plants. Another set of experiments, conducted by gynecologist and healer Leonard Laskow, demonstrated his ability to retard the growth of cancer cells through mind focus. In yet another experiment, Gene Barry, a physician-researcher in Bordeaux, France, successfully measured the retardation of a destructive fungus merely through the negative intention that was focused on it from a distance of 1½ meters.

It is clear that our *kavvanah* intention is a very real factor in our relationships with people and with the Cosmos at large. The way we focus through the *Yesod* flow can have a substantial influence on those who are either in our mind or with whom we are actually communicating at the moment. Negative thinking can redirect the *Yesod* flow in potentially destructive (as well as self-destructive) ways. Knowing this, we must seek to exercise both strength and sensitivity in the way we navigate across the interpersonal boundary. We must aspire to a positive disposition to life, to people, and to adversity.

The Bond of Love

Love has become a cliché. Western language abuses and misuses the term. It passes for the most facile of relationships, ones that are dependency ridden, promiscuous, and exploitative. We are encouraged by the media to accept as "loving relationships" the most superficial and mutually destructive emotional connections. We are encouraged to accept the least attractive attributes of the *Nefesh Behamit* as the reality of human love, rather than its distortion. Because of our terror of commitment, we choose to focus entirely on transient pleasures instead of committing ourselves to a *Yesod* foundation of love.

The crucible that forges true love is commitment and dedication to the spiritual, intellectual, emotional, and material welfare of the other. Love induces the bond. *Yesod* produces it. The *Sefira* of *Yesod* flows through everybody. No matter how repressed it might become, a loving relationship will allow the bonding process to arise and solidify.

The flow of *Yesod* encompasses both friend and stranger. How we treat our waitress, bus driver, or car mechanic is no less a statement of our capacity to relate than the way we express love for our immediate family, spouse, or close friend. Kabbalah teaches us to address people with our whole being—our total *kavvanah*. It is an indication of where our *Yesod* flow is being directed.

It should be noted that while love derives from our giving self, *Hessed*, it becomes manifested in the way we dedicate ourselves to another—the *Yesod* work of commitment. In the wonderful book called *Beyond the Best Interests of the Child*, Joseph Goldstein draws the distinction between biological parenting and psychological parenting. The difference lies in the element of commitment. The same is true of all love. The difference between biological love—sexual attraction—and the psychologi-

A STAR OF DAVID MEDITATION

Breathe in. Become aware of your senses. Recognize your taste buds by rubbing your tongue along your upper and lower teeth. Allow the scent of the room to penetrate your being. What sounds are entering your consciousness? What are your fingers touching? Where are your eyes focusing? Close them. Allow thoughts to pass through you gently with no prompting or urgency. You are safe. With your eyes closed, envision a beautiful lawn shaped like a huge six-sided Star of David. You are walking on the grass. You see your closest friend beckon to you, smiling. You immediately empathize with your friend's openness and warmth. Begin reflecting on your own capacities to be a giving and caring friend. Recognize your human capacities to infuse your compassion with the wisdom of Mind and the energy of Emotion. Spend a few seconds contemplating this.

cal love that comes from in-depth commitment is the flow of *Yesod*. When we commit ourselves to the very being of the one we love, we actualize our giving and compassionate natures.

A *Yesod* Exercise

1. When you do a daily task become aware of your five senses. For example, wash dishes: What's the sound the dish makes as it goes under the faucet? What does the dishwashing detergent smell like?
2. Become aware of your body as it engages in the job at hand. Is your body tense? Do your feet ache? How do your fingers feel? Take an inventory of your body and become aware of how you are inhabiting this moment in time.
3. Become aware of distractions. Ask yourself: "Why am I being distracted? How am I interpreting an essentially neutral moment? How am I filtering the moment?"
4. Ask yourself: "What is my emotional response to the distraction? Am I feeling resentment? Annoyance? Am I tired?"
5. Ask yourself: "How can I turn this subjective moment around?" For example, "Am I distracted by the neighbor who is playing his music loudly? How can

I turn the moment around so that it does not destroy my concentration and appreciation for the moment? What can I do to enhance my moment of *Yesod*?"

The Bond of Mindfulness

We are familiar with the idea of living in the moment through the teachings of philosophers like Thich Nhat Hanh. There are infinite moments in the spectrum of time. We race along, trying to catch an experience here and a moment there. In our frenzy to experience all of life, we experience precious little of the diversity and richness of the universe.

When we learn how to live in the moment, we bond with that moment. Think about it. At any given moment we are occupying some space. Our body, mind, and emotions are never in "no-space." But we are inattentive to the moment. When we become conscious of the way we connect with that moment, in that space, we can appreciate its singularity. The moment will never be repeated. We have an opportunity to create a unique occasion out of this never-to-be-repeated moment.

When we are present in the "now" we become spiritually enlarged and enriched. We become mindful of the absolute holiness that the moment possesses. We must train ourselves to be aware, for in reality we are where our mind is. Once again it is the facility of *Yesod,* the dedication, that enables us to touch the uniqueness of the moment and open up vistas of opportunity that otherwise would have eluded us.

Hassidism teaches us that all moments are special.

In the present moment lies the secret of both past and future.

This singular moment is both an expression of the way we lived in the past and an indication of the future. The way we engage the present determines the outcome of the future.

The Paradigm of *Yesod*

Sefirotic flows intermingle and merge into a conscious reality through the medium of *Yesod.* In the same way, the legacies of Abraham, Isaac, Jacob, Moses, and Aaron become funneled through the spiritual quality of Jacob's son Joseph.

Joseph is called the "perfect master"—the *tzaddik.* The *Tanya* teaches that one uniquely special *tzaddik* exists in the world at any given moment—the spiritual foundation of the world.

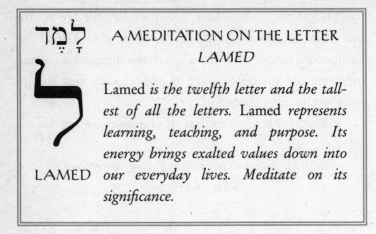

לָמֶד

A MEDITATION ON THE LETTER
LAMED

LAMED

Lamed *is the twelfth letter and the tall-
est of all the letters.* Lamed *represents
learning, teaching, and purpose. Its
energy brings exalted values down into
our everyday lives. Meditate on its
significance.*

The Bible tells us that Jacob gave his beloved son
Joseph a coat of many colors. This coat represents the
Sefirotic array of colors that Joseph was destined to funnel into the world. The Bible also reveals that Joseph
saved his father and brothers from starvation. The
Kabbalah tells us that this alludes to the manifestation of
the other *Sefirot* through the medium of *Yesod*.

Joseph was a dream interpreter, and a dream is a con-
nection between the conscious and the subconscious.
Yesod is the connecting point between the inner Mind-
Emotions and their ultimate expression through the
Sefira of *Malchut*.

Joseph, the paradigm of *Yesod*, became the foundation of the survival of the Hebrews. In the same way,
Yesod enables the *Sefirotic* flow to survive in conscious
reality.

14

❧

Malchut:
Into the World

Completing the Cycle

Malchut completes the cycle. It is the last element in a chain of events that begins with a moment of inspiration and finds its actualization in the real world—the world of the finite. Without the *Malchut* flow we would possess thoughts and feelings but never actualizing them.

Imagine planning a summer vacation. You book plane tickets, buy necessary clothing, and sweat through a fitness program. Then just as you are about to leave you discover the air traffic controllers have gone on strike. The Cosmos experiences our behavior in the same way when we fall short of our good intentions. The Creator must then rebalance the Cosmos to provide new opportunities for our follow-through. Some call this process karma or kismet. Kabbalah calls it *hashgacha pratit*—the opportunity that is designed to match our spiritual needs.

The Nature of *Malchut*

Malchut is an unusual *Sefira*. It has two spiritual characters. Like *Bina*, *Malchut* is feminine in nature. It carries in its womb all of the *Sefirot*, including *Bina*, to full term. *Malchut* is the end that appears in the beginning. It is the womb in which the spiritual flows of *Chochma* through *Yesod* nest before their birth in the real world.

Kabbalah calls *Malchut* the *Imma Tata'ah*—"the Lower Mother." *Malchut* nurtures the upper nine *Sefirot* until the moment of their manifestation as a word or behavior. It is the Lower Mother in contrast with *Bina*, the *Imma Ila'ah*—"the Higher Mother," in whose womb the upper *Sefirot* of *Chochma* and *Bina* were nurtured.

Malchut is also the *Alma D'Itgalya*, "the Revealed World." Here our latent potential is actualized through behavior and expression. *Bina*, on the other hand, is called *Alma D'Itkassaya*—"the Hidden World"—since the union of *Chochma* and *Bina* produces only a *potential* behavior, a Mind state. In the metaphor of the human body, *Malchut* represents the mouth, since the mouth speaks, revealing what is inside.

Thus far we have explored the *Sefirot* in terms of human behavior to enable us to grasp these complex notions more easily. But the *Sefirot* flow through the entire Cosmos, so the idea of *Malchut* actualizing inspired thoughts and emotions is also descriptive on a Cosmic scale. In fact, *Malchut* is synonymous with *Shechina*, the feminine presence of G-d in the world. It is the *Shechina* that funnels the waves of creative potential into a revealed, finite world. Note the anthropomorphic account of creation begins with the words "And G-d said, Let there be light." The *shechina* is manifest through a created world.

> *Malchut* is the highest spiritual source of souls
> and angels.

Although angels and human souls are distinct from each other, both evolve from the creative process that flows through the *Sefira* of *Malchut* in the highest world of *Atzilut*.

Here on Earth

The Kabbalah teaches humanity to be involved in the details of life. We are told not to remain aloof. A life spent in deep contemplation, removed from the material aspects of life, misuses the purpose of our existence.

Hassidic masters teach us that the merest word or action can create a change of immense proportions in the Higher Worlds (*Olamot*). Thus each of has a real responsibility to think, speak, and behave in an ethical manner. The universal *mitzvot,* the Seven *Noachide* Laws, are guiding principles for a moral and just society. We effect change in the world through action, not simply kindly thoughts.

Judaism has an *extensive discipline* of
6 1 3 *mitzvot-good deeds*-to *guide us*
through the *challenges* of life.

The world has a *complex system*
of 7 *mitzvot-good deeds*-
to *actualize* the Divine potential.

Malchut—The Sovereign State

Literally translated, *Malchut* means "Sovereignty." *Malchut* is derived from the Hebrew word for "king"— *melech.* Subjects may never get to catch more than a glimpse of their king in real life, but they can sense the royal presence through laws and the manner in which he is spoken about and obeyed. In the same way, *Malchut* is a passive but powerful state of being, as well as a more active and final state of actualization. Kabbalah teaches that *Malchut* gives us a glimpse of the divine sovereignty in the world.

Many metaphors are used to describe *Malchut.* It is seen as the container into which all other *Sefirot* flow. It is the final integration of our Mind-Emotion activity. *Malchut* is the sovereign state that exists within each of us. Through our speech and behavior others can glimpse the sovereign power that rules us.

Who we are is revealed in what we do.

Fulfillment Costs Less Than You Think

One of the truly great Chabad Hassidic masters, the *Rebbe* Yosef Yitzhak (known in the Lubavitch Hassidic school as the *Frierdicke Rebbe*), pointed out that the really necessary things in life are in inverse proportion to their actual cost. Jewelry, he noted, can be outrageously expensive. It can be worth the value of several homes. That is why jewelry is not essential to the maintenance of life. A dwelling, on the other hand, is far more necessary and, therefore, considerably cheaper than the best jewelry. Clothing, being more necessary still, is even more affordable. Food, being an essential, is cheaper than clothing. Water is even more basic to life and therefore costs even less than food. And that which comes free of any charge is the most essential of all—the air we breathe.

This simple guide provides us with an important yardstick. Many people spend years wandering the world, searching for happiness and fulfillment. But they may be looking in the wrong places. The elusive prize lies in the simple and inexpensive: someone to love, someone with whom to share one's life, someone to care for, someone to help bear the painful moments in life, and someone in whom to believe.

When we master *Malchut* we gain fulfillment. Stephen Covey says, "We address that which seems urgent, but never attain that which is truly important." Kabbalah tells us to allow the right mix to flow into our container of *Malchut*.

QUESTIONS TO ASK AT THE END OF EACH DAY

1. Did I do today what I truly believe to be important?
2. Have I worked this day toward my real goals?
3. Am I fulfilling my true aspirations?
4. (If the answer to any of these questions is "no") Why haven't I made the time?

Living in the Zone

Recently a number of books have explored the phenomenon known as "playing in the zone." Tennis players describe games in which their body responses were perfectly matched to their intentions. Writers describe working for hours on end in euphoric oblivion. Scientists describe being so engrossed in an experiment that they lose a sense of the passage of time, miss meals, and are unaware of noise and interruptions. These represent extraordinary states in which the flow of will configures the *Sefirot* so that they are manifest through *Malchut* in a higher consciousness. Once experienced, the phenomenon is never forgotten. Some of us may experience it as a mystical feeling of oneness and unity, when everything and everyone seems part of an organic whole.

A STAR OF DAVID MEDITATION

Breathe in. Become aware of your senses. Recognize your taste buds by rubbing your tongue along your upper and lower teeth. Allow the scent of the room to penetrate your being. What sounds are entering your consciousness? What are your fingers touching? Where are your eyes focusing? Close them. Allow thoughts to pass through you gently with no prompting or urgency. You are safe. With your eyes closed, envision a beautiful lawn shaped like a huge six-sided Star of David. You are walking on the grass. Feel its soft lushness. Find yourself walking on a jetty looking at the deep blue sea. Identify with the ocean's bold, even heaving as it breathes its ponderous waves. Take time to feel its immense depth and strength. Identify with that strength of purpose. Spend some time contemplating the image of the sea. Breathe its fresh, pure, strong essence. You are lifted up by a breeze. Find yourself resting lightly on a huge rose petal. Feel its softness and gentleness. The

breeze lifts the petal lightly, and you feel the sensation of its inner life—its symbiotic relationship with nature. Sense its power to grow, to bloom, and to close. Note your own power to develop, grow, and spiritually mature. Identify with the flower. You are the flower.

Continue walking. From a distance you spy a lion. Notice its majesty and regal bearing. It glides along, oblivious of you. Recognize its courage. Identify with the lion. Become aware of your own majesty, your own regal bearing, in the domain of the kingdom of your Mind and Emotions. You too can be the king of your spiritual jungle. Contemplate this for a moment. As you walk along the beautiful lawn, you see your closest friend beckon to you, smiling. You immediately empathize with your friend's openness and warmth. Begin reflecting on your own capacities to be a giving and caring friend. Recognize your human capacities to infuse your compassion with the wisdom of Mind and the energy of Emotion. Spend a few seconds contemplating this. Think about the archangels as you walk. You sense Michael walking on your right, showering you with compassion. Gavriel walks on your left, providing you with direction and purpose. The archangel Oriel walks in front of you, bringing inner enlightenment. Refa-el walks behind you, strengthening your own healing capacities. Spend a minute sensing the angelic forces imbuing you with their goodness and gifts. Now begin walking along the final corner—the Shechina corner. Allow yourself to merge with the Star of David. You become aware that you are the Star and it is also you. Recognize how your soul is the spiritual umbilical cord that connects you to the heart of the Star—to its very center and core. You are connected to the core. You are an outgrowth of the core —a projection of infinite worth onto the screen of time and space. You are one with the All. Spend a minute connecting to the All.

When We Come to the End
We Will Find the Beginning

Gandhi said that we must *become* the change we seek in the world. This echoes the Kabbalistic teaching that we are each a reflection of the whole Cosmos. Each lifetime we start from where we ended, and we end where we will start. The *Sefira* of *Malchut* is the end. It is also the begin-

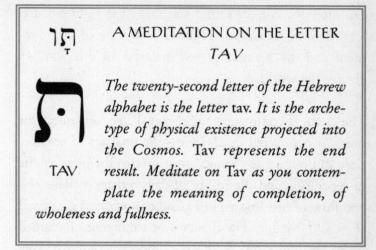

A MEDITATION ON THE LETTER
TAV

TAV

The twenty-second letter of the Hebrew alphabet is the letter tav. *It is the archetype of physical existence projected into the Cosmos.* Tav *represents the end result. Meditate on* Tav *as you contemplate the meaning of completion, of wholeness and fullness.*

ning. All ten *Sefirot* flow in each of the four parallel worlds of *Atzilut, Beriya, Yetzira,* and *Assiya.* The lowest *Sefira* in *Atzilut* is *Malchut,* but *Malchut* becomes *Keter,* the highest level of the *Sefirot* in the next world of *Beriya,* and so on. Imagine four ladders, one on top of the other. The bottom rung of the upper ladder becomes the top rung on the ladder below it.

The ultimate purpose of engaging in personal growth and development is to enable us to say the right word at the right moment and to engage in the appropriate act when we are called upon. Our blood, sweat, and tears; our hours of introspection; our journal keeping, meditation, breathing techniques, and exercise—all exist so we can utter the correct sound and make the right gesture. This delicate procedure requires a lifetime of improvement and the practice of self-mastery. In this way we change the world.

The circle is complete. Our raison d'être, our quest for unity, is completed in *Malchut*—the final act of connection. But our sense of unity gives way to the physical life of separation and the reality of daily existence. This ebb and flow of life, known in Hassidic thought as *ratzo* and *shuv,* is inevitable. The elements of a moment of attained unity become a gift in the next moment of separation. Seeds of the end are planted in the beginning, and in the beginning is the germ of ending.

Conclusion

I SET OUT TO WRITE a book that would serve as a bridge between the ancient and cryptic wisdom of Kabbalah and the contemporary inquirer. A bridge is useful only if it connects the two sides. To that extent I am aware that these ancient insights have to transcend time and place, extending to the Emotions and Mind of the reader today.

The result is, I hope, a "middle way" that is neither too technical nor simplistic. It wasn't written for the scholar or aspiring sage, but for people like myself who seek to improve the daily experience of living truly and honestly.

Daily each of us must commit to a pattern of words and actions. On one level our choice has impact on the very Cosmos. On another, more immediate level, our decisions determine the fabric of our lives. Before we close, I would like us to share an important teaching of

Kabbalah that can help us in a practical and down-to-earth way. I am speaking of its teaching concerning anger.

Counselors frequently advise their clients to "release" their anger, as though it were a caged animal that needed to be exorcised. On the other hand, they also point out that anger is a perfectly natural feeling. The Hassidic explanations of Kabbalah teach that anger is neither "locked up" nor natural. Releasing it only makes it stronger. In fact, the sages teach that anger has no redeeming qualities whatsoever.

The ancient spiritual traditions of Hinduism, Buddhism, and Judaism all regard anger as destructive and proscribed. And if we are prepared to borrow from these traditions in so many other ways, why ignore the teaching on anger?

Maimonides advises to always choose "the middle path" and to avoid extremes. Yet one of the exceptions he cites is in the case of anger. In this instance he advises angry people to practice the virtual opposite—passivity in the face of provocation. In his code of Jewish law called *Mishneh Torah* (*Hilchot Deot*, chapter 3), he writes: "Anger is an exceedingly bad passion, and one should avoid it to the last extreme. One should train oneself not to be angry even for something that might justify anger."

The *Tanya* goes even further and states that whoever

expresses strong anger is practically worshiping idols, because in the very moment of anger his faith has completely departed from him.

In part 2 we explored Emotions in terms of seven basic and concise *Sefirot*. Anger is not on this list. Kabbalah views anger as a "hybrid"—it is a product, not a raw spiritual material. For anger to be expressed, the Mind flows of *Chochma* and *Bina* have to interpret a situation through the workings of the ego self—the *Nefesh Behamit*. The *Da'at* factor has to elicit emotions, with a controlling emotion of *Gevurah* predominating, resulting in a defensive or offensive stance. The *Yesod* flow has to commit a dominating *Netzach* to stem the perceived threat. Finally, *Malchut* has to express the words or behavior of anger.

We can control our anger if we understand its ego and fear base, learn to intervene, and practice to offset its manifestations. But let us first understand how undesirable it truly is. Physiologically the expression of anger correlates with unhealthy side effects. Angry people are associated with type A behavior, which can result in heart failure. Anger raises the heart and pulse rates. Body organs malfunction in the ongoing climate of anger. Anger inhibits the immune system, raising susceptibility to infection and disease.

Anger is also socially disruptive. It aggravates interpersonal bonds and strains relationships. It is used as a weapon of control and domination. It precipitates distancing and fears. Angry people lose friends and have a poor influence on people.

Often you will hear people point out that anger is motivational. They will relate their pet story of someone they know who was so motivated by anger that it spurred him or her to high achievement. But hate is also motivational. So is jealousy, mistrust, inferiority, and tribal sacrifices to please the gods. Motivation per se is not a value.

This leaves us with the argument that the expression of anger allows us to "vent" unhealthy "pent-up" emotions. But is anger ever "pent-up" and somehow "trapped" in the body?

We have seen that Emotions are seven spiritual flows that are directed by the three flows of Mind. Nothing is trapped—it is simply a case of personal mismanagement when wisdom and self-mastery are lacking. Yet some people will swear that hitting the bed a hundred times with the broom brings them relief—or, better still, hitting someone on the mouth. They tell you that they "get it out of their system."

We have the capacity to create our own realities. Earlier we saw mind-body studies that illustrate how our belief system effects actual changes in our body chemistry, even to the point of affecting our immune system. Beliefs also form mind images.

If we believe that anger is "locked up" in the container of the body, then this will create a sense of inner pressure. Hitting the bed a hundred times with a broom "releases" that pressure *because we believe in our imagery and create that reality.*

Similarly, punching someone in the face for being nasty will also bring relief. But the price is socially exorbitant. And it is based on an unfounded belief—that it gets rid of anger.

Angry people continue to display anger long after it has been "vented." After rather short-lived relief, the only reality is that the broom-beaten bed needs replacing or the punched-in face lands the aggressor in jail.

Releasing pent-up anger is a belief based on a fiction. The relief is a temporary mirage, to which the next instance of anger readily testifies. The only way to eradicate anger is to understand its spiritual dynamic and learn, patiently and with practice, to change that dynamic so that the outcome is more appropriate, more pacific, and in the spirit of bonding and connection. This will result in true and permanent inner change, as the *Sefirotic* flows assume new and better patterns. An inner climate can be created where the Mind guides the Emotions.

To achieve this outcome, beliefs about anger must

change. We cannot imagine an "enemy" trapped within. It must be transformed into an image of the Mind and Emotion flows. We must become so familiar with the nature of these *Sefirotic* flows that we can conjure up an image of *Chochma* reformulating the *Bina* flow, and *Hessed* blending *Gevurah* more powerfully. These visuals will create powerful Emotion changes and neutralize the anger response.

Hassidism defines this process in the principle "Mo'ach shalit al halev"—the Mind shapes and defines the Heart. To fully comprehend how to practice this dictum necessitates another book. Let us wait and see.

Kabbalah is practical, and its knowledge is universal. The insights provide a model that is as comfortable in Western psychology and Eastern mysticism as it is in Jewish spiritual practice. It excludes no one through religion, spiritual pathway, or belief. It speaks to the soul, and each soul will respond according to its appropriate orientation.

It is my sincere hope that this book will be of assistance to you in your everyday life. I would warmly welcome your comments and further suggestions. Do feel free to be in touch with me.

I have enjoyed this journey with you. You have been a fine companion.

Glossary

An asterisk indicates a cross-reference in this glossary. All non-English entries are Hebrew unless otherwise indicated.

ahavah
> The Emotion of love, a subset of the *Sefira* of *Hessed*.

Alma D'Itgalya (literally "the Revealed World")
> A Kabbalistic synonym for the *Sefira* of *Malchut*, where the potential latent in the upper *Sefirot* is actuated in *Malchut*.

Alma D'Itkassaya (lit. "the Hidden World")
> A *Kabbalistic* synonym for the *Sefira* of *Bina*, so called because the *Sefirot* of *Chochma* and *Bina* produce only a potential feeling and expression that is not actuated until *Malchut* operates.

anivut
> The quality of humility.

Assiya (lit. "Making")
> The fourth realm, or **Olam;* the realm of time, space, and human consciousness.

Atzilut (lit. "Emanation")
> The first of the four realms, or **Olamot,* which for all practical purposes is indistinguishable from the Source, of the light of **Ein Sof.*

avodah, also *avoido* (lit. "work")
> Effort and practice of spiritual refinement.

Ba'al Shem Tov (lit. "Possessor of the Good Name")
> Founder of **Hassidism* (1698–1760, central Europe); "spiritual" grandfather of the founder of the **Chabad *Lubavitch Hassidic* movement.

ba'al teshuva (lit. "possessor of the path" or return)
> A person who has returned to the pathway of **Torah* practice.

Bar Mitzvah (lit. "the Son of the Holy Commandments of the **Torah*")
> The age of potential spiritual maturity for a male at the age of thirteen; a year later than the age of spiritual maturity, twelve for a female, called *Bat Mitzvah.*

beinoni (lit. "in between")
> A person who masters his or her actions and outward expressions while being aware of occasional inner turmoil and temptation; spiritually positioned between a master and a wicked person.

Beriya (lit. "Creation")
> The second of the four realms, or **Olamot;* the realm of spiritual individuality and distinctiveness.

Bina (Lit. "Understanding")

Second of the ten **Sefirot;* the spiritual aptitude for developing the thought source into a cogent thought flow.

bittul (lit. "annulment")

The process of ego abnegation.

Chabad

Acronym formed by the initial letters of the first three **Sefirot* through which intellectual activity is performed; the name of the **Hassidic* movement also known as the **Lubavitcher* movement

Chassid, see *Hassid*

Chassidism, see *Hassidism*

Chessed, see *Hessed*

Chochma (lit. "Wisdom")

First of the ten **Sefirot;* the spiritual aptitude to draw the seminal thought from the subconscious.

Da'at (lit. "Knowledge")

Third of the ten **Sefirot;* the spiritual aptitude to draw Emotion into the flow of Mind—called *Da'at Tachton;* the spiritual aptitude to allow creative thought and thought sequence to enter into unity and balance—called *Da'at Elyon.*

Derush

The third level of depth in understanding the **Torah;* the derivative level of understanding the **Torah* texts.

Ein Sof (lit. "Without End, Infinity")

The infinite source of creation; G-d.

Elokim

The name of G-d that is associated with the divine attribute of self-containment within nature and within the corporeal world.

emunah

Faith in the beneficence and purposefulness of creation; faith in G-d.

Gevurah (lit. "Strength, Heroism")

The fifth of the ten *Sefirot,* the spiritual attribute of restraint and self-containment.

gilgul (lit. "cycle")

The process of reincarnation of the soul.

Habad, see **Chabad**

hashgacha pratit (lit. "personalized supervision")

The spiritual teaching that the Creator is specifically aware and involved in every finite event and life, creating situations that are always for ultimate benefit.

Hassid (lit. "one who is pious")

A follower of Hassidism.

Hassidism (lit. "Pietism")

Torah movement founded by the ***Ba'al Shem Tov** that popularized the teachings of Kabbalah as well as blending piety with joy and fervor; behavioral approach to the practice of Kabbalah.

Hessed (lit. "kindness")

The first of the seven *Sefirotic* flows of emotion, *Hessed* represents empathic giving.

hitbonenut (lit. "self-understanding")
  Contemplative meditation used extensively by members of the *Chabad Lubavitch *Hassidic movement.

Hod (lit. "Glory, Echo")
  The eighth of the ten *Sefirot, the spiritual attribute of empathy and providing comfort.

Imma Illa'ah (lit. "the Higher Mother")
  The Kabbalistic name for the *Sefira of *Bina in whose womb maturates the subsequent *Sefirot.

Imma Tata'ah (lit. "the Lower Mother")
  The Kabbalistic name for the *Sefira of *Malchut in whose womb is nurtured the upper nine *Sefirot.

Ivri (lit. "Hebrew")
  Name given to the descendants of Abraham; the "other-sider."

Kabbalah (lit. "Receiving")
  The body of mystical Jewish teachings; the fourth level of depth in understanding the *Torah.

Kav (lit. "line")
  The initial input of a ray of divine energy after the initial divine contraction known as *tzimtzum.

kavvanah (lit. "directed intention")
  Focused intention coupled with focus of Mind and Emotion powers.

keili (lit. "utensil"); pl. *keilim*
  The spiritual container that holds the *Ohr—the spiritual energy or "light."

Keter (lit. "Crown")

The antecedent to all of the *Sefirotic* flows, also referred to as the highest of all the **Sefirot;* source of the flows of will and pleasure.

kosher

Food that is assimilable by the Jewish soul system as defined in the *Torah and **Talmud.*

l'chaim (lit. "to life")

Drinking to the health and well-being of another; often voiced aloud in the process of having the drink.

levushim (lit. "clothes")

The outer "garments" of the divine emanations through which the emanation can become manifest in the **realm,* or **Olam,* in which it passes through.

Lubavitch (lit. "Town of Love"; Rus.)

Townlet in Russia that was the center of *Chabad *Hassidism from 1813 to 1915; alternative name of the *Chabad Hassidic movement.

Malchut (lit. "Sovereignty")

The tenth and final **Sefira,* which concretizes, in the world of **Assiya,* the interacting processes of the previous nine into human expression.

mazal

The flow of specific spiritual energy that animates the soul of all matter, vegetation, animals, and humankind; often used as an expression of congratulation, as in *mazal tov* (lit. "good *mazal*").

mekubal (lit. "the one who has been received"); pl. *mekubalim*

The traditional term for a Kabbalistic adept.

memalleh (lit. "filling")

The description of spiritual energy occupying the "space" of its spiritual container, as does thought occupy the spoken word.

merirut (lit. "bitterness")

Hassidic practice of self-reflection focusing on one's failings but with the intent of self-improvement.

mezuzah

The rolled and scribally written parchment extracting a passage from the Torah and usually placed in an ornamental container and affixed to the doorpost of all doorways in a Jewish home.

Middot (lit. "Measures, Personality Traits")

The seven **Sefirot* of Emotion.

Midrash

Literature from the third level, **Derush*, of the four levels of understanding the **Torah*.

Mishna (lit. "learning, repetition")

The first rendition of the oral law before its elucidation in the developed discussions known as *Gemarra*, which together with the *Mishna* is called the **Talmud*.

mitzvah (lit. "commandment")

A precept of the Torah that when acted upon connects the soul to the Creator in a more profound manner.

mochin dekatnus (lit. "smallness of brains")
Being small-minded or immature in the way that choice is exercised.

Moshe Rabbeinu (lit. "Moses, Our Teacher")
Moses, who accepted and taught the **Torah* at Mt. *Sinai* in front of several million Jewish people and other exiles from Egyptian slavery.

Moshiach (lit. "the Anointed One")
The Messiah who will bring peace and harmony to the world, rebuild the Jewish Temple, and bring all Jewish exiles back to Israel.

Nefesh, also see *Nefesh Elokit* and *Nefesh Behamit*
The level of the soul most integrated into the physical body and the last level to depart after death.

Nefesh Behamit (lit. "the Animalistic Soul")
The dimension of the soul that seeks the fulfillment of the physical body and initiates the drives toward body pleasures.

Nefesh Elokit (lit. "the G-dly Soul")
The dimension of the soul system that is utterly united with the G-dhead.

neshama
The generic term for soul; the third level of the **soul,* the spiritual source for Mind activity.

Netzach (lit. "Permanence; Victory")
Seventh of the ten **Sefirot;* the spiritual attribute of reaching out to another and entering into relationship.

niggun

> *Hassidic* song, usually a wordless melody, utilized by *Hassidim* for intellectual, emotional, and spiritual growth and strengthening.

Ohr (lit. "Light")

> A metaphor for the energy flow or emanation from the Creator or Source.

Olam (singular of Olamot)

> See *Olamot*

Olamot (lit. "Worlds")

> The four major realms of increasing *Tzimtzum* in which the divine emanations become increasingly hidden in more outwardly defined formats, or *levushim.*

oneg (lit. "pleasure")

> The highest source of human motivation and expressed as the primary flow of connectedness.

Pardes (lit. "Orchard")

> The term used for Jewish mysticism and specifically the Kabbalah; the four levels of understanding the *Torah.*

Peshat

> The literal meaning of a word or piece of text; the first level of understanding the Torah.

Rachamim

> The quality of mercy and compassion; identified with the *Sefira* of *Tif'eret.*

Rambam (acronym for Rabbi Moshe ben Maimon; 1135–1204)

Maimonides; a Renaissance-style scholar, philosopher, physician, mathematician, and Talmudist; author of the most extensive and authoritative codification of Jewish law known as *Mishneh Torah.*

ratzo v'shuv (lit. "running toward and returning")

The cyclical pattern of human Mind and Emotions oscillating between intensity and relaxation, usually applied to the intense activity of consciously connecting to G-d and then needing to return to a more relaxed norm before seeking to approach again.

realm(s)

The four *Olamot,* or worlds, that increasingly contract and condense the divine emanations hiding their truer aspects.

rebbe

Hassidic master; spiritual leader of a Hassidic dynasty; in contemporary times the Lubavitcher Rebbe, Rabbi Menachem M. Schneerson, was commonly referred to simply as "the *Rebbe.*"

Remez (lit. "Hint")

The second level of understanding the *Torah*—the allusive level.

ruach (lit. "wind, spirit")

The second level of the soul system—the level manifested through human Emotion.

Sefira (singular of *Sefirot*)

  See **Sefirot*

Sefirot (lit. "Emanations")

  The ten divine attributes that manifest through the four **worlds,* or **realms,* called **Olamot,* and which actualize in the lowest **Olam* as the ten aspects of personality consisting of Mind and Emotion.

Seichel

  The triad of **Sefirot* of Mind, viz. **Chochma, *Bina, *Da'at;* the nature of Mind.

Shechina (lit. "indwelling")

  The level of the divine presence that is manifested in the corporeal **realm;* the feminine quality of the G-dhead.

Sod (lit. "Secret")

  The fourth level of depth of understanding of the **Torah,* associated with the level of **Kabbalah.*

Talmud (lit. "the Learning")

  The teachings of the **Torah* at Mt. Sinai that were kept as an oral tradition until their redaction into written form known as the Talmud in the years 200 B.C.E. to 300 C.E. in the great Talmudic academies of the Middle East.

Tanya (lit. "It Was Taught" [Aramaic])

  The name of the leading and most systematic Hassidic text explaining the natures of the Cosmos and the human being according to the **Kabbalah,*

authored by the founder of *Chabad Lubavitch
*Hassidism known as the Alter Rebbe, the Tanya is
also known as Sefer shel Beinonim (the Book of the
Intermediate Aspirants) and Likutei Amarim
(Collection of Discourses).

teffilin

Phylacteries worn on the head and arm by adult
males, usually during weekday morning prayers as
two small black boxes housing a scribally written
parchment extracting a section of the Torah.

teshuva (lit. "return")

The process of returning to the *Torah norms; also
see ba'al teshuva.

Tif'eret (lit. "Beauty")

Sixth of the ten *Sefirot that blends the spiritual
Emotion of giving, *Hessed, with the attribute of
restraint, *Gevurah, culminating in a balance of the
two.

Torah (lit. "the Teaching or Light")

The Jewish way of life governed by the five books of
Moses and the oral law that elucidates it; the body of
law given to and taught by *Moshe Rabbeinu at Mt.
Sinai; the spiritual blueprints of creation.

tum'ah

Spiritual state of negativity and impurity.

tzaddik (lit. "the righteous one")

The Hassidic master; a very righteous individual.

tzimtzum (lit. "contraction, concealment")

The divine process of progressive self-limitation making possible the various stages of independent entities coming into being, culmination in the variegated existences in the finite world of the human being.

worlds

See **Olamot, *realms.*

Yesod (lit. "Basis")

The ninth **Sefira,* the spiritual attribute of determination and dedication.

Yetzirah (lit. "Formation")

The third **Olam,* or *realm, in which the spiritual form of the fourth **world* of **Assiya* is determined; name of the most ancient work of **Kabbalah* still extant—*Sefer HaYetzirah,* written by Abraham.

Zohar (lit. "the Shine")

The primary text of **Kabbalah,* redacted into written form by Rabbi Shimon bar Yochai in the second century C.E.

RABBI LAIBL WOLF

AUSTRALIA:

Email: spiritgrow@laiblwolf.com
PH: +61 3 9525 8770 (office)
        +61 3 9525 9004 (home)
FX: +61 3 9525 9003
Mail: 29 Murchison St.
        E. St. Kilda
        Victoria 3183 AUSTRALIA

USA:

Email: hdioffice@aol.com
PH: 773 267 4700
FX: 773 478 9650
Mail: 6150 N. Lincoln Ave.
        Suite 101
        Chicago, IL 60659
www.laiblwolf.com

*"As a face is reflected in water,
so do we reflect each other."*

The Author's Kabbalah Audio/Visual Self-Master/Growth Tools

Audio

GUIDED IMAGERY MEDITATION:

Awakening to a New Dawn: Moving from sleep to wakefulness through a posture of ego abnegation.

Achieving Inner Unity and Balance: Allowing the Mind and Emotion to become unified and balanced.

Activating Your Higher Self: Bringing wisdom into the moment of challenge and seeming adversity.

The Healing Light: Alleviating emotion and physical pain through positive focused transformation.

EMOTION GROWTH MEDITATION:

Transforming Anger: Rebalancing the spiritual *Sefirot* energies neutralizing anger and negative emotions.

The Flow of Love and Relationships: Drawing on the

deepest source of self to enrich and deepen relationships.

COPING WITH STRESS—THE RELAXATION RESPONSE:
Relax and Breathe with Laibl: Breath based focus realizing a creative life and conscious awareness.

TREE OF LIFE ENERGIES:
The Ten Sefirot—*the Tree of Life:* Systematic analysis of the *Sefirot* as expressed in the human personality.
The Celestine Principles and Kabbalah: Comparison of the Nine Insights of the Celestine Prophecy and Kabbalah.

INNER SPACE AND THE HIGHER REALMS:
Angels, Souls, and Dreams: What are true Angels? How do they relate to the Soul? What is the nature of Dreams and how can we use meditative endeavor to dream more truly?

Video

Mysticism and Kabbalah No. 1: Introduction to themes and concepts in Kabbalah mysticism and meditation.
Mysticism and Kabbalah No. 2: Further themes and concepts in Kabbalah mysticism and meditation.

Inquiries and Orders

NORTH AMERICA & NORTHERN HEMISPHERE:
PH: (773) 267 4700; FAX: (773) 478 9650
email: hdioffice@aol.com
MAIL: 6150 N. Lincoln Ave., Suite 101, Chicago, IL
60659, USA

AUSTRALIA & SOUTHERN HEMISPHERE:
PH: +61 3 9525 8770; FAX: +61 3 9525 9003
email: spiritgrow@laiblwolf.com
MAIL: 29 Murchison St., E. St. Kilda, Victoria 3183,
Australia

Index

Index

Barry, Gene, 202
bar Yochai, Rabbi Shimon, 7, 17
beauty, in *Tif'eret*, 158–59
belief, power of, 107–12
Benson, Herbert, 107–8
Beriya, 36, 56, 57, 59
Bet, meditation on, 97
Bina, 61, 82–99
    as *Alma D'Itkassaya*, 210–11
    in *Chabad*, 166
    cord of many colors, 84–86
    flow exercise in, 94–96
    in human metaphor, 165, 166
    as *Imma Ila'ah*, 210
    inner balance of, 149
    integration of *Chochma* and, 99
    male and female in, 86–88, 210
    and Mind, 84
    and mind plasticity, 90–92
    quantum of, 86
    right and left brain activity in, 88–90
    in table of three pillars, 161
    and understanding, 104, 150
    visualization exercise, 98–99
    yellow color of, 84
bond:
    of love, 202–6
    of mindfulness, 206–7
    true, 197–208
brain, right and left, 88–90
breath:
    of creation, 34
    as metaphor, 34
    nature of, 23–24
    see also meditations
Buber, Martin, 170–71
Buddhism, Eastern traditions of, 21

cave, 7–8
Chabad, 166
Chabad Hassidism, 13
change, four keys to, 4–6
cheshbon nefesh, 5
Chochma, 60, 67–81
    blue color of, 84
    in *Chabad*, 166
    ephemeral nature of, 73–75
    fishing metaphor of, 68–72
    flow exercise in, 74–75
    in human metaphor, 165, 166
    inner balance of, 149
    inner duality in, 76–81
    integration of *Bina* and, 99
    light in, 72–73
    male and female in, 86–88
    and Mind, 84
    quantum of, 86
    reinterpretation in, 67–68, 83
    right and left brain activity in, 88–90
    in table of three pillars, 161
    thought exercise in, 71–72
Chopra, Deepak, 147–48
colors, 84–86, 92
communication, 181–85, 201
compassion:
    flow of, 150–53
    universal goal of, 8
consciousness, 35–38
consciousness exercise, of *Da'at*, 110
correlation, nonlocal, 200–1
Cosmos:
    and person, 115
    as reflected in each of us, 218–19
    teaching of, 157
Covey, Stephen, 183, 214

Index

Index

Index

Index

About the Author

LAIBL WOLF (RABBI), LL.B., M.Ed.Psych, is an internationally renowned lecturer in the fields of mind and emotion mastery and personal growth. He has been invited to lecture in 165 cities in the past five years alone, indicating the reputation and wealth of experience, not to speak of stamina, that he possesses. He has founded the Human Development Institute, a foundation dedicated to the progress of humankind through insight and personal mastery. Being one of the few traditional exponents of *Kabbalistic* teachings, while having studied law and psychology as well, he combines the wisdom of the past with a modern and progressive view of the present.

He has appeared extensively in the media and been keynote speaker at international conferences, including those of the International Psychological Association, the International Transpersonal Association, the International Mind/Body/Immunity Conference, and the American Orthodox Union of Rabbis.

He has produced an extensive set of self-mastery and meditation audiovisual materials that are available on four continents. These explore the teachings in a more experiential manner, and have the advantage of the author's emphases as well.

He resides in Melbourne, Australia, with his wife, Leah, and their three younger children.